£15.00

Local Government Briefings

Abolition or Reform?

Local Government Briefings

1   The Case for Local Government
    George Jones and John Stewart

Abolition or Reform?

The GLC and the Metropolitan County Councils

NORMAN FLYNN
London Business School

STEVE LEACH
Institute of Local Government

CAROL VIELBA
Polytechnic of the South Bank, London

London
GEORGE ALLEN & UNWIN
Boston   Sydney

George Allen & Unwin (Publishers) Ltd,
40 Museum Street, London WC1A 1LU, UK

George Allen & Unwin (Publishers) Ltd,
Park Lane, Hemel Hempstead, Herts HP2 4TE, UK

Allen & Unwin, Inc.,
Fifty Cross Street, Winchester, Mass 01890, USA

George Allen & Unwin Australia Pty Ltd,
8 Napier Street, North Sydney, NSW 2060, Australia

First published in 1985.

British Library Cataloguing in Publication Data

Flynn, Norman
    Abolition or reform: the Metropolitan Counties and the GLC. – (Local
    government briefings; 2)
1. Greater London Council
I. Title   II. Leach, Steve   III. Vielba, Carol
IV. Series
352′.0094′0942   JS3623
ISBN 0-04-352119-3
ISBN 0-04-352121-5 Pbk

Library of Congress Cataloging in Publication Data

Flynn, Norman
    Abolition or reform?
(Local government briefings; 2)
Bibliography: p.
Includes index.
1. Greater London Council. 2. London Metropolitan Area (England) –
Politics and government.
I. Leach, Steve.   II. Vielba, Carol A.   III. Title.
IV. Series
JS3625.F55   1985   352.0421   84-24384
ISBN 0-04-352119-3 (alk. paper)
ISBN 0-04-352121-5 (pbk.: alk. paper)

Set in 10 on 11 point Times by Fotographics (Bedford) Ltd
and printed in Great Britain by
Billing and Sons Ltd, London and Worcester

Contents

Introduction

The government is committed to the Conservative Party general election promise to abolish the Greater London Council (GLC) and the metropolitan county councils (MCCs). This commitment, although hastily made, was not to be deflected by internal dissent or defections of members of the House of Commons or the House of Lords. Margaret Thatcher said in 1979: 'It must be a conviction government. As Prime Minister I could not waste any time having any internal arguments' (quoted in Keegan, 1984). The proposed reform of local government is unlike previous ones; it has emerged without detailed analysis of the present system and the possible alternatives.

Opponents of the proposals have not accepted the abolition as inevitable. They have used the parliamentary channels of lobbying and persuasion as well as public campaigns to win popular support, including the four by-elections caused by resignations of Labour members of the GLC. This book has been written in the belief that debate about the future of local government is necessary and useful. While we are not necessarily supporters of the existing structure, we do believe that it is important to understand how that structure developed and to evaluate its performance, before changing it. When the abolition proposals were announced we were engaged on a research project, funded by the Economic and Social Research Council, into the working of the two-tier local government system in England. This research has formed the foundation for much of this book.

A superficial interpretation of the current proposals is that they simply result from political antagonism between the MCCs and the GLC and the government. While it is correct that the Conservative Party has been annoyed, especially by the use made of his position as GLC leader by Ken Livingstone to berate the government, it is unlikely that the government has felt threatened. The abolition proposals have their origins in the growing tensions between the institutions of local government and the apparatus of central government. The proposals should be seen as an attempt by central government to gain further control of local government, rather than a series of adjustments within local government in London and the metropolitan county areas. This centralization is part of a long-term trend towards a reduction in local autonomy and should be seen together with the Rates Act 1984, which gives the government control over rate levels as a further important step along the road towards a completely unitary state within which a single set of policies are pursued. The present government has pursued a strategy of attempting to reduce public expenditure, to limit public provision of services by encouraging private provision, and redirecting the efforts of government towards defence and law and order. This stance has broken the postwar consensus on social policy since it conflicts with policies adopted by many local authorities.

The GLC and the MCCs were conceived as government units which had certain overall responsibilities for their areas and were charged with the provision of particular services. The design of the system was flawed by the boundaries adopted and by the distribution of functions. These flaws were not the accidents of inexperienced designers but the result of the political and social forces which produce the institutions of the state.

Despite the design, these local government machines have been operating for a decade in the case of the MCCs and two decades in the case of the GLC. Judgement of the design can, therefore, be made in relation to the performance of these institutions and not solely on the basis of their design principles, although a decade or two is a short period over which to judge.

The White Paper (Department of the Environment, 1983) which proposed the abolition argued that conflict between the MCCs and the district councils was inevitable. We have found that the degree of conflict has been exaggerated and that in any case the conflicts have often represented the clash of interests which exists in the metropolitan areas rather than competitive struggles between self-seeking local government bureaucracies. These clashes of interests will be expressed within any system of government.

We decided to assess the MCCs' and the GLC's performance in service delivery and found that, although expenditure per head may be higher for services provided by these authorities, this may reflect a higher standard of service. As strategic authorities the GLC and MCCs had some successes but these have been limited by the ambiguity over the upper-tier authorities' role, the fact that political control changes frequently and by continuous interference from central government. Conflict between the tiers of local government represents differences in interest and ideology which will not be removed by the removal of the GLC and MCCs: they will reappear as conflicts among the boroughs or districts or between them and the government.

When we turn to the future government of the metropolitan areas we find that there are two extreme models for local government as a whole: a system in which central government makes all the policy and service choices and local authorities merely administer the services locally or a system of local autonomy where central government takes on only those tasks which cannot be done at local level.

There are also possible forms of intermediate government between the centre and the basic unit of local government.

When we look at the interests which are served by these models we can predict what sort of governmental system is likely to be established. In addition to this fundamental choice there is also the question of the type of local government unit which is likely to be established. Here the basic choice in the urban areas is between a system which groups within an area the people who have different interests and one which segregates them. The conflicts which arise from those different interests can be expressed either within or between units of government. If they are to be expressed between units there is then the question of where the resolution of those conflicts takes place; whether there should be an intermediate level of government between the locality and central government.

A reform of local government needs to face these choices. The current, hurriedly constructed proposals are presented as an improvement on the existing system, in that local government will, it is claimed, be more efficient, comprehensible, accessible and accountable if they are implemented. A two-tier system of local government certainly has its problems, but a system consisting of a host of joint boards and joint committees, backed by a range of central government controls, all superimposed on the existing district tier, hardly justifies the White Paper's title, *Streamlining the Cities*.

This book is an attempt to examine critically the government's view of the existing MCCs and the GLC, and its proposals for changing the system of metropolitan government, in the light of the available evidence.

Local Government Briefings

Abolition or Reform?

1 The Abolition Proposals

> I believe we have got progressively to return to the concept
> that the GLC is a strategic authority.
> (Patrick Jenkin MP, letter to the Secretary of the Marshall
> Inquiry on Greater London, 1 August 1977)

Streamlining the Cities

In October 1983 the Department of the Environment published a
White Paper called *Streamlining the Cities* which outlined proposals
to implement the government's manifesto commitment to abolish
the GLC and the MCCs. It proposed to distribute the functions
currently carried out by those councils either to the lower tier – the
London boroughs (LBCs) or the metropolitan district councils
(MDCs) – to combinations of councils acting through statutory joint
arrangements, or to other bodies, including central government
departments. The White Paper also set out the proposed constitution
and powers of the joint boards which were to be the bodies through
which the lower-tier authorities would run police, fire and public
transport outside London, fire throughout London and education in
inner London. Consultation on the proposals was carried out through
consultation papers which were written and issued after the White
Paper. After this process considerable changes were made to the
proposals.

The abolition of the GLC and the MCCs was the starting-point for
the White Paper and the subsequent amendments, not the
conclusion. We were reminded by a senior civil servant responsible
for the production of the White Paper that the present government
does not proceed from analysis to conclusions, but from commitment
to action.

The arguments for abolition presented in the White Paper were
based on the need for economy in public administration and the lack
of 'practical' role for the upper tier in the metropolitan areas. Figures
were presented which were said to show that the expenditure of the
upper tier had been excessive and that there was now a climate which
did not require the strategic role with which those authorities were
charged when they were established. A distinction was made between
the arrangements in the metropolitan areas and those prevailing
outside. Because the upper tier in the shire areas was responsible for a
larger proportion of the total of local government spending than that

of the upper tier in the cities, their justification for being retained was seen as being self-evident. It was implied that the justification for retaining a local authority followed from the number and type of services provided and the proportion of overall local government expenditure for which the authority was responsible. Hence, had the county councils in the metropolitan areas been responsible for, say, education and social services (as in Scotland) then the case for their retention would have been stronger.

Because of the lack of a clear strategic role, the White Paper argued that the MCCs had been seeking to establish a role for themselves. This search had inevitably led to a conflict when the lower tier, responsible for the delivery of most services, disagreed with the strategic assessment made by the upper tier. Conflict between the tiers should, therefore, result in the abolition of one of them. This argument goes to the heart of the nature of the system of urban governance. If there are indeed issues which need to be resolved at a spatial level larger than the individual boroughs or districts and if there is conflicting interest between, say, inner city and suburban authorities then there will inevitably be conflict. In such cases where there are real material conflicts and the resolution involves one party winning at the expense of another, then the organization which achieves the resolution is bound to be in conflict with the loser. In fact in the case of the MCCs there have been few issues over which there has been a genuine material conflict. Policies which favour inner cities have largely been central government sponsored, through the Inner City Partnership Programme or other inner city arrangements. In those cases where a redistribution of resources has been made, such as in the case of highways maintenance expenditure, the abolition of the upper tier does not remove the inherent conflict, it merely allows a different winner to emerge. In so far as it has been the case that the upper-tier authorities have been able to redistribute resources in a strategic way to favour poorer or Labour-controlled areas, the removal of the strategic tier will prevent that redistribution.

The White Paper states that the reorganization represents a reallocation of functions to the lower tier:

> The Government believe that most of the functions at present exercised by the GLC and MCCs should become the direct responsibility of the borough or district councils. (para. 1.18)

Annex B of the White Paper sets out the proposals on the allocation of functions (see Appendix 1). Although a majority of the *functions* are proposed to be transferred to the borough and district councils, the majority of the expenditure of the existing upper tier is proposed to be transferred to 'Statutory Joint Arrangements'. In the metropolitan county areas these include police, fire and public transport. In London the White Paper also proposed a statutory joint arrangement for education for inner London, although this proposal was later withdrawn and replaced by a proposal for a directly elected Inner London Education Authority. The proposed arrangements are joint boards consisting of members of the lower-tier authorities nominated in such a way as to reflect the political composition of the nominating authorities. In London the joint board for the fire service was to be one representative of each borough council and one from the Common Council of the City of London. The boards would operate as independent legal entities with the power to hold property, incur debt and precept on the constituent. However, for the first three years 'the precepts issued by each joint board should be subject to approval by the appropriate Secretary of State' (para. 6.6).

For those functions which required co-operation between the district or borough councils but which were not to be governed by joint boards, the White Paper proposed 'to leave it to those authorities to co-operate voluntarily as necessary' (para. 2.2). If such co-operation was not forthcoming the secretary of state expected to intervene on planning matters where structure plans conflict with those of neighbouring authorities or with national or regional policies (para. 2.7), on highways and traffic management and on waste disposal, where reserve powers would be held.

The proposals as set out in the White Paper were followed by a series of consultation papers which provided more details of the proposed arrangements. These papers disclosed, more than the White Paper, the degree to which central government control and influence over the transferred functions would be exercised. The consultations produced over 1,300 replies and resulted in many amendments to the proposals. The amendments reflect two things: the desire to placate opposition from particular interest groups, such as the arts lobby, and the fact that the proposals were assembled in a great rush. The main features of the original proposals and the major amendments to them are as follows.

Planning

The White Paper proposed that the structure planning function would be transferred from the GLC and the MCCs to the lower-tier authorities. In addition, it was proposed that the secretary of state would issue 'guidelines for the review and preparation of individual structure plans by each of the borough or district councils in that area'. In London a London Planning Commission was proposed which would advise the secretary of state. The secretary of state proposed to take powers to 'ensure that, where appropriate, structure plans are brought forward simultaneously . . . and will require those plans to be submitted for his approval only if, for example, they appear to conflict with national or regional policies or with the plans of neighbouring authorities' (para. 2.7).

The consultation paper added the proposal that planning conferences, chaired by a representative of the regional office of the Department of the Environment (DoE), be established outside London. In the detailed proposals published at the end of July a statutory planning conference for London was also to be established. Structure plans would continue, with their production co-ordinated by the secretary of state who would, if necessary, issue group commencement orders to ensure that the plans were produced at the same time. Structure plans were to be 'short policy statements' which would 'set out no more than the main land use policies for the area of the plan, to enable the Secretary of State to satisfy himself that the plan is in accordance with national and regional policies and to provide an adequate context for the provision of local plans' (DoE, Consultation Paper: The Reallocation of Planning Functions in the Greater London Council (GLC) and Metropolitan County Council (MCC) Areas, para. 18).

This proposal was later amended and a new type of plan was invented: 'The government have now simplified the proposals so as to provide for a new type of unitary development plan tailor-made for the LBCs and MDCs as all-purpose planning authorities' (Department of the Environment, 1984, para. 2). This new type of plan would consist of two parts: the first part would be for the planning authority's general policies; the second would contain the authority's specific proposals. In other words, the structure plan is subsumed as a part of the unified plan. The secretary of state would issue guidance which could include all the major elements of any plan, including the general level of provision of housing, major transport links, the general level of provision and the locations for major new commercial or industrial development and overall policies on Green Belts, agricultural land, mineral extraction and 'other matters as appropriate' (ibid., para. 6).

The White Paper also proposed to transfer the GLC's responsibilities on historic buildings to the London boroughs but after vociferous lobbying the GLC's Historic Buildings Division was kept intact by a proposal to transfer it to the new Historic Buildings and Monuments Commission. It would be preserved as an entity within that organization.

Public Transport

The White Paper proposed that public transport in the metropolitan areas should be run by joint boards, which would be similar to the

Passenger Transport Authorities which were in operation before the creation of the MCCs. In addition it suggested that district councils should be allowed to operate their own transport services, as long as the arrangements were compatible with those made by the joint board for the whole area. It was also indicated that private operators might be able to contract for public transport services directly with the district councils. The joint boards would be responsible for major decisions on fares and service levels, but the fact that they were to have their precept approved by central government would limit their actual scope for policy choice.

Highways and Traffic

The White Paper simply stated that the responsibility for highways other than motorways and trunk roads would pass to the boroughs and districts. The consultation paper added that the government would like to see the maximum use made of private sector consultants and contractors (DoE, Consultation Paper: Reallocation of Transport Responsibilities, para. 9). The role of the regional offices of the Department of Transport was also spelled out: 'There may also be a case for considering whether it would be appropriate for the Department of Transport to take over the preparation of certain major new highway routes in metropolitan areas' (para. 11), and 'Regional Offices will have an important role to play in helping to determine priorities for financial resources ... and in helping to resolve occasional differences between district councils. Where agreement cannot be reached it is for consideration whether the Secretary of State will need reserve powers to carry out the necessary work' (para. 13) and 'In London it is proposed that the borough councils should notify the Secretary of State in advance of certain categories of proposals (i.e. lorry bans, bus priority, parking and permanent lane restrictions . . .' (para. 17).

Thus even in a service which in the White Paper appeared as a straightforward transfer of a function to the boroughs and districts the detailed proposals are in fact a transfer of strategic matters to the regional office of the Department of Transport. In London it is far more than strategic matters which are transferred. The idea of the secretary of state being responsible for bus lanes and parking restrictions goes beyond any definition of strategic.

Waste Regulation and Disposal

The White Paper transferred these functions to the boroughs and districts and called for voluntary co-operation between the authorities, with a reserve power if this co-operation was not forthcoming. In the Consultation Paper these proposals stood but a new element was added: the possibility of extending the participation of the private sector. Privatization was considered, not simply for contracting out the provision of disposal sites (which is fairly common current practice) but also 'The employment of a private contractor or a consortium of contractors, perhaps on a management fee basis, to plan, organize and implement waste disposal arrangements under the direction of the responsible local authority or authorities' (DoE, Consultation Paper: Arrangements to be made for Waste Disposal, para. 13). This issue, while completely extraneous to the concerns of the White Paper, may provide a clue to a possible hidden set of objectives in the proposals. Patrick Jenkin told the Institute of Wastes Management Conference on 5 June 1984 that cost-effective solutions 'must involve a major extension of private sector participation and investment. . . . The private sector must grasp the opportunity with imagination and flair. . . . I want our proposals for reorganization to be seen as a major opportunity to secure the real advantages that competition brings.'

Housing

The White Paper simply dealt with the transfer of the remaining GLC housing stock to the boroughs. The Consultation Paper on housing dealt with the problems of the GLC Seaside and Country Homes and the Greater London Mobility Scheme which allows transfers between boroughs. For both of these, voluntary co-operation was called for, not only between London boroughs but also between boroughs and the district councils to which the GLC schemes outside London were to be transferred. Any future arrangements for the construction of dwellings outside London should be made by 'transferring resources to the host District Council in return for nomination rights to the dwellings concerned' (DoE, Consultation Paper: Housing, para. 10).

In the case of the remaining large GLC holding of dwellings, Thamesmead, the boroughs were asked to make proposals about who whould take over the stock. The DoE recognized the difficulties which some of its proposals may cause, but asked for indulgence: 'it is recognised that a number of these proposals relate to detailed matters of administration in which the Department has had little direct involvement' (para. 20). Even when the detailed proposals were published at the end of July 1984 the question of Thamesmead had not been resolved, although by then an independent trust was being considered.

Support for the Arts

Originally the government expected the boroughs and districts to take over the GLC's and MCCs' contribution to the arts. There was opposition from the arts lobby to this proposal. For example the Arts Council felt that boroughs and districts would be less generous towards the arts than the MCCs and the GLC because of competing demands on resources from 'pressing social needs, or the need to maintain statutory services at an adequate level, and of central government pressure to contain . . . their total spending' (quoted in *Guardian*, 8 February 1984). The response to the arts lobby was to establish a £34 million fund for the arts; £16 million would be distributed through the Arts Council of Great Britain, £17 million would be for major museums and art galleries, and £1 million would be for the British Film Institute.

Although the £34 million was mainly a way of placating a lobby it raised an important matter of principle: because it was considered likely that districts and borough councils might consider other demands on their resources more pressing than the need to subsidize the arts, central government intervened to ensure the continuation of arts support.

Fire and Police

The reorganization of the fire service was relatively simple in the White Paper. As with the police service outside London the fire service would be controlled by joint boards comprised of members of the borough and district authorities while the existing brigades would be maintained 'on both operational and cost grounds' (DoE, 1983, para. 2.19). Even this simple formulation was amended. On 4 May Patrick Jenkin announced:

> We have decided to provide in the main Bill for the possibility that individual authorities or groups of authorities could be permitted to take over responsibility for fire and police services in their areas, provided that the authorities concerned can demonstrate, once the joint boards have been in existence for a reasonable time, that they could administer the services more effectively and that provision nationally and in the rest of the metropolitan area would not be adversely affected.

This really is a most extraordinary proposition. A new set of institutions is to be established, but if district councils can show that they could do better they will be allowed to make a bid for taking over the service in their own area. Since any particular bid would affect the whole of the police and/or fire service, this implies that after a 'reasonable time' another reorganization would be in order.

Education

The biggest U-turn occurred over the future of the Inner London Education Authority (ILEA). The White Paper stated:

> In order to secure that education policies are developed within the context of the totality of demands being made on inner London ratepayers, the Government propose that the new single authority should be a joint board composed of elected representatives nominated by the inner London borough councils and the Common Council. The new authority would thus be based on the boroughs. (para. 2.20)

On 5 April the Secretary of State for Education, Sir Keith Joseph, announced that in fact the new authority would be directly elected, because 'the nature, scale and importance of the education service in Inner London taken together, justify a directly elected authority in this special case'. However, Sir Keith also announced that the Bill would contain a power to abolish the new authority, depending on its performance.

It was not made clear what particular criteria applied to ILEA which did not also apply to, say, the public transport service in the West Midlands or the police service in Greater Manchester. The case of ILEA does indicate, however, that the proposals were subject to change according to the strength of the lobby and illustrates that there was not firm commitment to the details of the proposals, but rather a commitment to the abolition itself. The White Paper was concerned with the removal of the GLC and the MCCs rather than with devising arrangements for services which would produce an effective local government system. If it is the case that the government is more committed to abolish than to reform local government, then it is important to examine why this is the case.

Why did the government decide on abolition?

During 1982 a Cabinet subcommittee, chaired by William Whitelaw, looked into the possibility of abolishing the MCCs and the GLC. The subcommittee, code-named MISC 79, was trying to balance the administrative upheaval which would be caused by such a measure against the political gain from abolishing what it saw as unpopular councils. MISC 79's main remit was to find a way of abolishing the domestic rates since this was a long-standing aim of the Conservative Party and of Mrs Thatcher. It failed in this latter task, mainly because the most obvious alternative to domestic rates was a local income tax which was politically unacceptable to a party committed to tax reductions. The subcommittee produced a report in January 1983 which it felt would satisfy the party and Mrs Thatcher, despite not meeting previous commitments on the rates. It proposed the abolition of MCCs and the GLC and a new form of rate relief for single householders.

Meanwhile, the Treasury had been arguing that the government's controls over local authority spending were inadequate, the influence over the spending of particular authorities contained in the Local Government Planning and Land Act 1980 (and the subsequent powers taken by the Secretary of State for the Environment) had not curbed the high-spending councils, and direct control was felt to be needed.

When the general election was called a decision had to be made about what to include in the manifesto on local government. In the absence of any politically acceptable alternative to the domestic rates, the Cabinet needed some positive measures and accepted Leon Brittan's proposal to control rate levels (a proposal known as 'rate-capping' and now enacted in the Rates Act 1984) and MISC 79's proposal to abolish the MCCs and the GLC. The abolition would be presented as a measure which would reduce bureaucracy, duplica-tion and waste. The title of the subsequent White Paper *Streamlining the Cities* was to carry this message. Abolition of the GLC would have the added bonus of 'wiping Ken Livingstone, his group and his administration off the face of the earth and certainly off the front page of the *Standard*' (Pauley, 1984, p. 74).

Although the proposals in the manifesto were decided in haste and without detailed consideration of the implications, they had their roots in a history of conflicts between the government and the Labour-controlled MCCs and GLC. Ken Livingstone, the current Leader of the GLC, argues that the government had been looking for ways to abolish the GLC from the moment the Livingstone group took office: 'Simply the cutting of fares and the setting up of the Enterprise Board was enough to persuade the government that we should be abolished – our desire to build houses was considered revolutionary' (Ken Livingstone, interviewed by C. Davies-Coleman, *Municipal Journal*, 29 June 1984, p. 980). Policies pursued by the MCCs with regard to fares and economic development were also contrary to central government philosophy and policy. In general the Labour-controlled GLC and MCCs were in opposition to central govern-ment's policy to reduce public expenditure in the face of the recession. These authorities opposed that policy and believed in a public-expenditure-led recovery of the economy.

Some MCCs, following the lead given by South Yorkshire, made a strategic assessment of the nature of urban transport which gave emphasis to public rather than private transport for passengers. The upper-tier authorities were responsible for public transport and for large parts of the major highways networks. They were, therefore, in a position to implement a strategy which limited investment in highways and produced continuing revenue support for bus and rail operations which would incur operating deficits at the fares required to attract passengers away from cars on to the public transport network. It was central government policy to reduce the operating deficits by charging higher fares. Central government used various mechanisms of grant support to try to impose its policies on the local authorities with, from its point of view, a disappointing degree of success.

A second issue over which there had been tension was the interventionist role adopted by various authorities including the GLC and many of the MCCs in relation to the local economy. Although the development of the economy and the encouragement of the creation of jobs was not a specific statutory responsibility for the local authorities there were various powers under which such activities could be undertaken. Under the Inner Urban Areas Act 1978 various grants and loans could be made to companies in designated inner areas. There was also a general power under Section 137 of the Local Government Act 1972 to undertake activities which were to the benefit of the people of the area. Many authorities, including MCCs and the GLC, made use of this power (see Crawford and Moore, 1983) to develop policies to respond to the impact of the recession on the cities. These policies came into conflict with the response to the recession of central government which expected the recession to force cost reductions through competitive pressures. If these pressures failed to improve unit costs in companies then they would be forced out of business and be replaced by more efficient companies. The various efforts of the local authorities have been directed towards helping the survival of companies in order to maintain the level of employment in their areas. In some cases the Enterprise Boards which have been established have carried out policies which have attempted to exert political influence on the operation of private companies. The Planning Agreements signed between, for example, the West Midlands Enterprise Board and companies receiving help have included commitments about the numbers of jobs to be retained and about the employment policies with regard to equal opportunities to be pursued by the companies. Although small in their overall impact on the economy, or on the level of employment, these approaches to the relationship between the private and public sectors were in direct contradiction to central government's declared attitudes and policies.

As police authorities, some MCCs have been in conflict with the Home Office over the style of policing to be adopted, particularly in the inner city areas. They have challenged decisions on equipment to be issued to police forces such as riot shields and plastic bullets, and have questioned the relationship between the police and black people. These challenges have been seen by the government as 'political interference' into its policies of law and order.

Many Labour-controlled authorities, including the GLC and some MCCs, had also introduced redistributive elements into local politics. Disadvantaged sections of society were offered special help. Women and black people especially, but also residents of deprived areas, have been identified as requiring assistance. Welfare rights has been taken up as an issue by several MCCs and grants have been made to groups representing the disadvantaged, in an effort to promote their interests. At the same time, MCCs and the GLC have declared their areas 'nuclear-free zones' in protest against the development of nuclear power and the deployment of nuclear weapons. These interventions, along with the policies towards the economy, were not envisaged in the Acts which established the local authorities and are in contradiction to central government policy.

Perhaps the most visible conflicts were between the government and the GLC. In addition to the policy stances which the GLC has shared with the MCCs (including those towards the police despite the fact that the GLC was not a police authority) the GLC adopted a combative stance with the government. Ken Livingstone has become a prominent public figure, using his leadership of the GLC as a platform from which to challenge government policy across a whole range of issues from the economy to Ireland.

Patrick Jenkin has expressed the Conservative Party's concern with the stances taken by Labour-controlled local authorities. He told the party's local government conference in April 1984 that the 'hard left' were seizing control of local authorities: 'In many areas we now face the full-time professional politicians of the hard left. This is the new front line.' Central control of local government and the abolition of seven Labour-controlled authorities may be seen as an attempt to deny the 'hard left' the opportunity to control local authorities. However, the tendency towards increasing central control over local authorities has a history which predates the recent emergence of the new left in local government and the new right in the Conservative Party.

The trend towards centralization

The proposed abolition of the MCCs and GLC is the latest in a series of changes in the relationship between local and central government. If we take a long-term view we can see the transfer of employment exchanges, electricity production and health services from local authority control to single-purpose organizations accountable to central government as the start of the process of centralization. More recently, the government has attempted to reduce the importance of local authority housing provision through policies of giving local authority tenants the right to buy their homes and by switching housing resources to housing associations. Public transport in London has recently been removed from local authority control. The transfer of powers to single-purpose agencies accountable to central government weakens local authorities' powers and reduces their capacity to allocate resources among different services. The allocation of resources in London between, say, public transport and highway building cannot now be done by a single directly elected body.

Apart from the transfer of functions from local government to single-purpose bodies, central government has sought to increase its power and influence over local authorities. The government has tried to achieve council house rent increases by withholding subsidy from housing authorities which did not comply with its rent changes. The Manpower Services Commission is gaining increasing influence over the non-advanced sector of further education which is still nominally under local authority control. The Department of the Environment has been involved in a large number of major town planning issues. Legislation has been introduced to establish control over direct labour organizations which local authorities use for building and highway maintenance. In all these areas of local authority service provision there has been increasing central government interference and a reduction in local autonomy.

The most important shift towards central control over local government has been the move towards central government imposing expenditure decisions on local authorities. The Local Government Planning and Land Act 1980 produced a new mechanism for allocating central government grants to local authorities. The grant distribution system was to be used to influence those authorities which spent at levels higher than the government's assessment of the need to spend to provide a standard level of service. The grant percentage was reduced for those authorities which spent in excess of the government's assessment. When it was apparent that this influence was not strong enough to realize the government's plans, a new system was introduced which set targets which were based on the reduction of the volume of expenditure below the levels attained in 1978/9. Since 1981 grant has been progressively withheld from those authorities which spent at levels in excess of the target for volume reductions set by the government. The Rates Act 1984 allows the secretary of state to determine the rate levy, and therefore the expenditure level of any authority which wishes to spend in excess of his assessment.

Given that the secretary of state has taken power to control the expenditure levels of any local authority, it may be thought unnecessary to abolish the GLC and the MCCs on the grounds of excessive spending. The Rates Act powers allow that spending to be controlled. The abolition itself could not have been conceived as a way of making significant expenditure savings unless only a very superficial appraisal was made. No work was done at the Department of the Environment on assessing the possible savings. We were told that such work was not possible in the abstract and not until the White Paper proposals were produced could such an estimate be made. In the House of Commons claims were made by Tom King about the projected savings but these were not supplied by civil servants. Patrick Jenkin has said that the savings would be substantial, although this claim did not satisfy the British Chambers of Commerce, who commented in April 1984, 'Only if evidence of real savings in costs is forthcoming can the continued support of the business community be counted on' (quoted in *Sunday Times*, 8 April 1984). Various estimates have since been produced, although none has been published by the Department of the Environment. The estimates conflict. A study commissioned from Coopers and Lybrand by the metropolitan county councils concluded that the annual change in costs would be between a saving of £4 million and an additional cost of £61 million (Coopers and Lybrand Associates, 1984). A study produced by some district council officers in the West Midlands predicted significant savings in cost. The validity of these predictions is not what is important here. What is important is that no clear cost savings were apparent when the decision was made. No functions are to be abolished completely, they are simply to be redistributed. Some duplication will be eliminated but in a limited range of services accounting for a small proportion of expenditure. Accumulated debt charges will remain to be paid by the successor bodies. If cost reductions are achieved it will be because central government control of the precepts of the joint boards ensure that savings are made.

The precedents are not auspicious. Recently a tier of administration was removed from the National Health Service. What appears to have happened is that most of the work and staff of the Area Health Authorities have been transferred to the District or Regional authorities with very little financial saving but with a great deal of disruption.

It would appear, then, that cost saving was not the most important motive behind the abolition proposals. They are part of a tendency for central government to establish control over local authority activities. What remains to be explained is why this increased desire for centralization in the face of conflicts between central and local government should have arisen now.

The breakdown of consensus

If there was agreement between central and local government about the actions which the latter should take, there would be no need for central government control. Recently there has been a breakdown in the national consensus about economic and social policy, as economic growth slowed after the 1973 oil crisis and reversed in the post-1979 recession. During the first three postwar decades there was a degree of consensus between the political parties about the management of the economy and the nature of the welfare state. There was an agreement that there should be state provision of housing, health, social services and education. Full employment would be achieved through economic management and that economic management would include the expansion of the level of public expenditure as a counter-cyclical measure. During this period there was a steady development of the services provided by local government. The postwar reconstruction of the housing stock especially in the cities included a large amount of local authority house-building. Education was expanded. There was a growth in the number of public sector employees, including those employed in local government. Following the 1973 oil crisis and the agreement reached with the International Monetary Fund on the management of the economy and public expenditure the consensus between central government (responsible for economic management) and local government (responsible for the delivery of many of the services) began to break down.

During the period of growth there was no strong opposition from business interests to the expansion of the public sector. It was a part of the consensus that the provision of education and welfare and infrastructure was a necessary condition for the promotion of economic growth. Local authorities, the main institutions through which these services were provided, were not directly controlled by representatives of the business community (and particularly not representatives of large companies) because there was no need for that degree of intervention. Some local authorities were, therefore, able to pursue policies which may have gone beyond the interests of business and represented the interests of deprived people, working-class people or, indeed, the authorities' own employees. There can be little doubt that during the period of local authority (and other public sector) expansion, there were significant gains for the professional and other workers engaged in providing the services and some gains for the people receiving the services. These groups had taken advantage of the fortuitous circumstances prevailing to pursue their interests. To the extent that this process produced a relatively autonomous local authority sector, those who opposed its growth were forced to use political power at the national level to defend their own interests.

It is that pressure to reverse the tendency towards autonomy of local authorities from business interests which has created the lobby for central government control. Central control over rate increases protects the business ratepayers against the local authority's demands. The Manpower Services Commission will provide through the further education sector training which is relevant for business. The removal of general housing subsidy makes house purchase more attractive, which is good for private house-building. Business interests are now represented through central government and its control over local government, because local government has in many cases ceased to act in the interests of business, at least in the cities. This representation is apparent not only in the general direction of government policies towards local government but also in specific actions, such as the introduction of the requirement (in the Rates Act) to consult local business before setting a rate. Pressure from business to reduce the burden of rates has resulted from the fact that as company profitability has fallen, rates have increased as a proportion of profits. Between 1960 and 1975 non-domestic rates as a proportion of gross trading profits increased from 9·5 per cent to 38·4 per cent (Dunleavy, 1980, p. 63).

Unfortunately for local government, the shift from a policy of expanding the public sector to one of stabilization, along with the emergence of monetarist economic policies, came in 1975, the year after the reorganization of local government outside London. New authorities were created in an atmosphere of growth and optimism which was soon dispelled by both economic and political pressures. Since 1979 those pressures have intensified. Local authorities charged with strategic intervention in the economic and social life of their areas came into conflict with the set of economic and political doctrines which emerged in the Conservative Party at the end of the 1970s. The new 'economic evangelicals' as Keegan (1984) has described them, believed in reducing the role of the state, both in intervention in the economy and in the level of expenditure. At the same time a shift in emphasis occurred in central government priorities. Local government, apart from the police service which was protected from expenditure cuts, was caught between the government's desire to reduce public spending overall, the need to increase social security expenditure because of the growth in unemployment, and the desire to increase spending on defence and law and order.

Apart from policing, the services provided by local government were mainly ones of low priority for the post-1979 administration. Meanwhile, the deepening recession had affected the metropolitan areas disproportionately hard, with unemployment rates in excess of the national average.

The city areas were faced with increasing problems, but also with a government committed to reducing both public expenditure and state intervention. By 1981 when the economic evangelicals had been in power two years all the MCCs were under Labour control, and many were controlled by politicians who believed in increasing state involvement in the private sector and disagreed fundamentally with the government's free market philosophy and its philosophy of rolling back the boundaries of the state.

In these circumstances a confrontation between central and local government was almost inevitable. The government's economic and social policies and its desire to represent business interests brought it into direct confrontation with those local authorities which represented different interests and which pursued different policies.

Legislation: the first hurdle

The first step in the abolition of the MCCs and the GLC was to cancel the elections which were due in May 1985, in order to clear the way for the new arrangements to take effect from 1 April 1986. There were two problems for the government. Parliament would have to be asked to approve the cancellation of the elections before it knew in detail what would replace the bodies to be abolished. Many MPs and Lords felt that they were being asked to approve the abolition proposals unseen, as well as the cancellation of the elections. The second problem was what to do about the services provided by the MCCs and the GLC between May 1985 and April 1986. Two options were available: the sitting members could be allowed to remain in office for a further year or they could be replaced by interim councils from May 1985 to April 1986. If the sitting members were allowed to remain, the Livingstone administration would be allowed almost a further year in office. If interim councils were set up, consisting of district or borough council members, the political control of London and some of the metropolitan county council areas would change, without an election being called. Initially Patrick Jenkin favoured the first option, of allowing existing members to remain until the abolition, but seems to have come under pressure from some Conservative back-benchers to get rid of Ken Livingstone in particular as quickly as possible. In September 1983 he wrote to the Prime Minister recommending that substitute authorities be established as an interim measure because 'both our own supporters and the wider public would find it incomprehensible that we should, in effect, extend the terms of the GLC and the MCCs' (quoted in *Guardian*, 30 June 1984). Despite objections from Mrs Thatcher, this was the proposal which the Cabinet accepted and which was written into the Local Government (Interim Provisions) Bill.

These measures produced a revolt by back-bench Conservative MPs, including Edward Heath, Francis Pym, Ian Gilmour and Geoffrey Rippon. Mr Rippon said that it was 'abject, squalid and shameful that a Conservative government should come forward with a proposal to substitute a directly elected socialist authority, which I would like to see the back of, by an independent, nominated quasi-quango of another political party'. An amendment calling for an inquiry into local government in London and the metropolitan areas was supported by 17 Conservatives but was defeated by 135 votes, and one allowing the existing members to stay in office was defeated by 142.

In the Lords there was a revolt against the proposals. The Lords were also concerned with the constitutional implications of replacing an elected authority by an appointed one with a different majority. The Bishop of Wakefield said: 'I think we are in danger of going down a rather slippery slope if we create precedents in Parliament of entrusting ministers with such far-reaching executive powers – and in this case the power to cancel elections involving a quarter of the English electorate.' The Bill was rejected in the House of Lords which approved by 191 votes to 143 an amendment which delayed the cancellation of the elections until after the Abolition Bill had been approved. However, the defeat proved to be a minor setback. The Lords failed to pass an Opposition measure to ensure that the 1985 elections took place (it was defeated by 248 votes to 155) and then passed without a vote an amended Bill which abolished the elections and allowed the existing members to sit until April 1986.

This revised measure then left Patrick Jenkin with the problem of how to control the reprieved authorities during the period leading up to abolition. He chose to do this by making it mandatory that the GLC and MCCs received his approval for any building and engineering works in excess of £250,000 and virtually any other item of expenditure over £100,000 during the interim period. These powers were contained in the Interim Provisions Bill. A further problem which he faced was that the GLC and MCCs may choose to transfer resources to the borough and district councils before they were abolished. On 24 July 1984 he announced his solution to this problem: 'I will seek, in the main Abolition Bill this autumn, Parliament's retrospective approval to a measure whereby all provision of financial assistance by the GLC and the metropolitan county councils to the London Boroughs, to metropolitan district councils or to any other local authority, will require my specific consent.' This announcement of the intention to pass retrospective legislation appeared almost a month after Mr Jenkin thought he had covered all eventualities with the Interim Provisions Bill. His handling of the affair did not make Mr Jenkin popular with Conservative back-benchers. John Wheeler, chairman of the Conservative London MPs group, told the *Local Government Chronicle*: 'The government has handled this issue so badly that it is on trial as far as Conservative MPs are concerned. Mr Jenkin must demonstrate that he can perform more effectively.'

The government's commitment to the abolition has not been shaken by these parliamentary events. The Lords' objection to the constitutional problem posed by changing political control of the GLC and the MCCs without a vote has been met by prolonging the lives of the existing councils. Its majority in the Commons is probably sufficient to ensure the passage of the substantive Bill despite objections by some Conservative back-benchers to what Edward Heath has described (see *Local Government Chronicle*, 1984) as a 'dog's breakfast of measures'.

2 The Evolution of Metropolitan Government

> It is axiomatic that anyone who speaks on local
> government reform, who does not have to, wants his head
> examining. Any government embarking on local govern-
> ment reform are likely to make more enemies than friends,
> both within their own party and on the opposite side of
> Parliament.
>
> (Harold Wilson, House of Commons, 6 July 1972)

Introduction

In this chapter the circumstances surrounding the major changes in
the structure of government in metropolitan areas since the Second
World War are examined, and the major features of the upper-tier
institutions of local government which resulted are discussed. In
attempting to comprehend the processes of change involved, a
number of different approaches have apparent potential utility. At
one level the story of local government reorganization since 1945 is a
story of influential individuals in positions of power, capable of
persuading colleagues of the need for change, even when the political
ramifications of the direction of change were obscure. At a second
level it is a story of objective analysis, undertaken by Royal
Commissions, into the problems of government in fast-changing
metropolitan areas and the use of such analysis to suggest logical
solutions to these problems. At another level, it is a story of political
opportunism, bargaining and compromise, making use of (and
partially constrained by) pressures from the major organizational
interests involved (individual local authorities, local authority
associations, professional associations, and so on). Finally, the story
may be viewed as one of a conflict of class interests (partly but not
wholly represented by major political parties) in a particular spatial
arena – the expanding conurbations. These interests may be seen as
being distributed unevenly within metropolitan areas so that the life-
chances of any one class will be variously affected by different
structures of metropolitan government. This class conflict may be
seen as underpinning although not wholly explaining the political
opportunism, bargaining and compromise mentioned earlier. This
level of analysis can in fact be extended to throw light on the overall
relationship between central and local government in a period of

economic crises such as the present. In such circumstances, the need for the extension of control of the former over the latter is viewed by certain class interests as a major priority in attempting to overcome the crisis (see Chapter 1, pp. 15–16).

The analysis in this chapter concentrates on the interplay between the first three of these levels – objective problems, political and organizational interests and the influence of key individuals – with the influence of class interests on the political stances taken being acknowledged where appropriate. In discussions about reorganization in the 1960s and 1970s, the argument that reorganization was needed to extend the control of local government by central government was certainly not overtly on the political agenda. Indeed it was the loosening of central controls and increased local responsibility which were stressed. It would be hard also to argue that this line of analysis had much relevance at more covert levels. However, it can be argued that most of the political and organizational conditions which enabled the major reorganizations of 1964 and 1974 to take place do not seem to be present in 1983–4. In attempting to explain current events, it is the final level of of analysis – the pressure for increased central control over local government – which is potentially more fruitful (see Chapter 1, pp. 15–16).

The main line of argument in this chapter may be outlined as follows. During particular periods, certain 'environmental pressures' have developed in our major conurbations, normally associated with the impact of economic growth (for example, population growth; competition for land; increased pressure for housing development; increased levels of car-ownership and commuting, and so on). Such phenomena may be regarded as 'objective' factors in the process of change, in that they are measurable, and their impact can be observed and experienced (and also because they are external to the process of change which is the main concern of this book). These environmental pressures impinge upon the existing governmental system in the conurbations (which has both 'local' and 'central' components), and tend to create 'institutional strain'; a mismatch between the scale and intensity of the pressures and problems caused by them, and the capacity of the governmental system to cope adequately with them. This mismatch may reflect *inter alia* difficult-to-resolve policy differences between different types of local government units (for example, the battles between Manchester and Cheshire over housing overspill in the early 1960s: see Lee *et al.*, 1974, ch. 2) and/or inter-agency power battles (for example, the 'Middlesex problem' in the 1950s; this was primarily about attempts by ten large and growing districts to obtain county borough status which, if granted, would have made the existence of Middlesex as a separate unit quite impossible: see Smallwood, 1965, pp. 98 ff.). Academics will draw attention to the environmental pressures and the lack of institutional capacity to deal with them. The local governmental institutions – at both political and officer level – will do so only if they feel that they can gain enhanced power or status, or solutions to the major problems as they perceive them, by so doing. Civil servants, particularly at the regional level, will be well aware of the environmental pressures and institutional strain, because they will have been used in a variety of ways as mechanisms for resolving them (for example, at planning inquiries) and may also exert behind-the-scenes pressure for change. Processes of change will, however, be initiated nationally only if influential politicians (which normally means a government minister or ministers), having weighed up the urgency of the problems and the political implications of change, can see significant benefits in doing so, and can so persuade their colleagues. The most likely alternative structures will already be well known, having been put forward and discussed in the academic local government world. The initiation of the process of change customarily involves the creation of an arena (Royal Commission, White Paper) in which the various interests express their views, form alliances, lobby and so on. The resulting proposals for change (or some modified form of them) will however then be implemented only if a pro-change coalition can be secured and sustained over the necessary period of time (which can be up to six of seven years) either through the fortuitous survival of the initiating government, or the acceptance of the need for change on a bi-partisan basis.

Thus in trying to make sense of the various attempts – successful or otherwise – to change the pattern of metropolitan government, three sets of forces must be borne in mind; first, the environmental pressures, already referred to, which are putting strain on the existing institutional arrangements; second, the politics of the existing institutional arrangements and the alternatives which are being canvassed (What is the pattern of political control in the existing system? How is it likely to change in the proposed alternatives?); and third, the views and relative power of the interests likely to be affected by change (especially local authority associations and professional institutions).

Underlying the stance taken by the major political interests involved will be an awareness of the social class implications of the existing situation and the proposed changes, both nationally and locally. Hence the Conservative Party will always be concerned about the impact of structural change on the farming interests in rural areas, and on business interests in urban and metropolitan areas. Similarly, the Labour Party will be concerned about maximizing its opportunities for power in the working-class areas from which it traditionally draws most support (for example, inner city areas, council estates and areas dominated by traditional primary and manufacturing industry). National perceptions may not of course always accord with local perceptions (for example, the strong probability of Labour control in Norwich may be accepted by the Conservatives nationally as a price to be paid for the retention of a Conservative-dominated Norfolk).

One of the interesting features of this description of the elements of the process is that although it is appropriate to the two recent changes in the structure of metropolitan government in London (1964) and elsewhere in Britain (1974) and the events leading up to them, and also helps explain the failure of other initiatives for change (Ullswater Commission, 1923; *Organic Change in Local Government*, Department of the Environment, 1979) it is much less helpful in understanding the current proposals for the abolition of the GLC and the metropolitan counties. Pressures for change in the metropolitan areas are *not* currently strong, either in terms of objective environmental factors (the problems associated with economic growth have, of course, reduced considerably since the mid-1970s) or with regard to 'institutional strain'. Here, although there are, as we shall see, difficulties in the operation of the two-tier system, and although some individual metropolitan districts and London boroughs have periodically campaigned for change (and are so doing currently), there is not at the moment a strong lobby for change from the units of local government involved. This is true also of the local authority associations and the professional institutes. There is no apparent civil service unease with the current system. Indeed in some regions, such as the West Midlands and Tyne and Wear, extremely good relations have developed between the Regional Offices concerned and the metropolitan counties (for example, over Inner City Partnerships: see S. N. Leach, 1981). Many customary features of the 'arena for the expression of interests' have been absent; no Royal Commission, very limited public debate over the (extremely thin) White Paper; a lack of readiness on the part of the government to respond to those affected by the proposed change, or influential outsiders. There is no coalition of interests in favour of the proposed change; or bi-partisan support for the need for it (see Chapter 1). Robin Pauley has written recently (see S. N. Leach, 1984):

Politics is all about power and that is all it is about. And if it is about improving anything or improving anybody's lot, that is necessarily secondary to its primary function which is to chase power, to gain it and then to hold on to it.

Whereas this view represents something of an overstatement with regard to earlier changes in the structure of metropolitan govern-ment, it does seem more appropriate to what is currently happening. A government with a large majority in the House of Commons is pushing ahead with change on the basis of a hastily written manifesto commitment and against the advice or wishes of almost all the other interested or disinterested parties!

An Historical Perspective

As a number of influential writers have pointed out, the debate about metropolitan problems and appropriate structural responses has been dominated by the example of London (see Young and Garside, 1982; Young, 1984a; Redcliffe-Maud and Wood, 1974). It was in relation to the growth of London in the nineteenth century that the idea of 'metropolis' first sprang (a metropolis can be defined as 'a conglomeration of distinct communities which are bound together by their dependence upon the labour market and commercial opportunities afforded by a central city', Young and Garside, 1982, ch. 10). It was with the most appropriate form of government for the fast-growing metropolis of London that much of the debate between the wars concerned itself (including the abortive Ullswater Commission which reported in 1923). It was in connection with London that there came the first major breakthrough in changing a structure of local government in metropolitan areas which had survived unscathed since the turn of the century, with the publication in 1960 of the Herbert Commission Report and subsequent (modified) enactment of its main recommendations in 1963. And it is the Greater London Council which has proved the major source of irritation to the current Conservative government, and the major reason for the government's determination to proceed with the legislation to abolish it (and the six metropolitan counties). Without the existence of the current manifestations of metropolitan govern-ment in Greater London, it is highly unlikely that the existence of the metropolitan counties alone would have been threatened (see Young, 1984a; Pauley, 1984).

In each of the periods preceding the recent major reorganizations of metropolitan government a number of similar conditions have been present which have reflected in one way or another pressures from the environment, the politics of reorganization and the balance of power amongst the major interests involved. In both cases, there was considerable strain on the existing institutional arrangements stemming from trends associated with economic growth. In both cases too there were considerable divisions amongst the various interests involved which were exploited by those eager to initiate non-incremental change. In each case there was a strong civil service lobby, particularly from the Ministry of Housing and Local Government (later the DoE) for a more 'rational' system of metropolitan government. While the period preceding the enactment of change in Greater London coincided with a period of unbroken Conservative control nationally, the period preceding the enactment of change in the provinces straddled periods of Labour (1966–70) and Conservative (1970–4) control at Westminster. In the latter case, the political implications of the proposed changes were open-ended enough not to preclude either of the two major parties accepting them (or some modified version of them); while in the former case, although the Labour Opposition opposed the legislative proposals strongly, the Conservative government managed to get the change implemented before Labour was returned to power in 1964. By then, the fact that the GLC and twenty of the thirty-two London boroughs were Labour controlled had diluted any residual Labour desires to repeal the legislation.

The Origins of the Herbert Commission

There were, however, significant differences in the relationship between environmental conditions and institutional strain, although this relationship acted as one of the major pressures for change in both situations. For a long time prior to 1957, when the Herbert Commission was set up, the fragmented system of government in Greater London had proved in a number of ways palpably inadequate to deal with the problems associated with metropolitan population and employment growth (see Young and Garside, 1982, chs 7–9). As Young has pointed out, the old London County Council (LCC) reached its peak population of 4·5 million in the census year of 1901. Thereafter it was the area outside the LCC boundary which grew most rapidly until in 1938 the population of the built-up 'outer area' equalled for the first time that of the inner area with around 4 million in each (Young, 1984a). Hence for several decades prior to 1957, the sprawling mass of metropolitan London had been governed locally by one 'inner metropolitan' county, covering a fairly arbitrary chunk of its inner area; twenty-eight second-tier metropolitan boroughs within this inner area; five county councils responsible for sectors of the outer area (and, in the case of Middlesex, wholly contained within it) containing around seventy second-tier municipal boroughs and urban districts, with assorted responsibilities; and finally three all-purpose county boroughs. The inability of this motley collection of around a hundred local government units to cope with the interrelated problems of a large metropolis has been underlined by a number of writers. The various 'advisory plans' produced for Greater London (notably Forshaw and Abercrombie's County of London Plan, 1943, and Abercrombie's Greater London Plan, 1944) were particularly influential in this respect. One commentator on the Abercrombie Greater London Plan wrote that 'nothing in the report is more important than this recognition of the complete futility of hoping there will be planning ... whilst the [existing] administrative jungle is not cleared up' (Phillips, 1945, p. 38). Young and Garside write of 'the problem of area-wide co-ordination in Greater London itself, where the multiplication of agencies bedevilled the provision of metropolitan infrastructure' (1982, p. 299). The growth of motor traffic and the notorious problems of London's roads steadily increased the pressure for some form of co-ordinated review of the Greater London area (ibid., pp. 284–5). The difficulties experienced by the LCC in solving its housing needs within its own boundaries and its problems in negotiating adequate 'overspill' sites within the predominantly Conservative-controlled outer area are also well-documented (Young and Kramer, 1978). Indeed, all these problematic aspects of metropolitan growth had been in evidence since the 1920s; yet no action was taken to provide a more appropriate governmental structure to deal with them until 1963. The mismatch between metropolitan growth problems and inadequate institutional arrangements cannot in itself explain changes in the structure of metropolitan government.

The phenomenon which most writers stress as being the most significant aspect of institutional strain in the Greater London area was not the effects of metropolitan population and employment growth *per se*, but rather the growing internal conflicts of the two-tier system in Middlesex and (to a lesser extent) Essex. Young (1984a, p. 3) emphasizes the importance of 'the need to find a special solution to the problems of Middlesex where the ambitions of large and powerful district councils (and in particular, "the big ten") to achieve county borough status threatened to make local government in the county unworkable'. This issue 'had been evaded by perplexed ministers and officials for years, yet seemed to be gradually worsening and could not indefinitely be shelved' (Young and Garside, 1982, p. 299). Smallwood (1965, p. 72) writes that 'by the mid 1950's it had become increasingly obvious that the county borough situation (in Middlesex) could not remain in a state of suspended animation for the indefinite future' and further argues that the then Minister of Housing and Local Government (Henry Brooke) left little doubt that the dilemma of the unresolved county borough problem in Middlesex had served as the key catalyst in forcing the decision to establish the Herbert Commission. Certainly this conclusion is supported by the amount of time and effort spent by the Commission on the problem of Middlesex. Young and Garside (1982, p. 299) also regard the 'long standing need to adjust the relationship between the LCC and the MB councils as a factor of some significance in initiating the process of change'. Thus the major impetus towards reform was not a social-class-based division. (The LCC and the London boroughs were predominantly Labour controlled; Middlesex and the 'big ten' alternated between Labour and Conservative, with the latter predominating.) It was rather a division based on *status*, with units, often of the same political persuasion, competing for existing powers.

The Origins of the Redcliffe–Maud Commission

In the provincial metropolitan areas, the equivalent of the 'Middlesex problem' was limited to the ambitions of only a limited number of authorities (for example, Solihull's ultimately successful bid for county borough status after the Second World War). The major institutional strain in these areas was that between the large county boroughs at the centres of the conurbations (especially Birmingham, Manchester and Liverpool) and the counties which surrounded them. The strain was most apparent in the running battles between Manchester and Cheshire, Birmingham and Worcestershire and (to a lesser extent) Liverpool and Lancashire over housing overspill. These battles were underpinned by political differences (the cities were normally Labour controlled; the counties always Conservative) and reflected the resistance by the middle-class and farming interests on the conurbation fringe to the intrusion of working-class council estates into areas of high residential amenity and agricultural quality. The arenas for these battles were the numerous 'public inquiries' over specific overspill sites, or proposals for new or expanded town development schemes in the 1950s and 1960s. However, on balance the Redcliffe-Maud Commission's Report laid more stress on the 'objective' environmental factors which (in its view) required a 'metropolitan tier' in the major conurbations to tackle them effectively – the growing interdependence of conurbation and surrounding countryside, as increasing car-ownership widens the scope for residential choice; the housing needs of the major cities and their inability to meet them within their boundaries; and the growing interdependence of work, home and leisure activities in the conurbations and their rural hinterlands. Indeed, it was a concern with devising a system which could respond adequately to such problems (but which was not too remote from the population) which led the Commission, in certain metropolitan areas only, to depart from its underlying principle of unitary authorities. 'Where, however, planning problems have to be tackled as a whole over an extensive area containing a very large population, as is chiefly to be expected in a great urban conurbation with its surrounding territory, to make a single authority responsible for all local government services would put too heavy a load of work on it' (Redcliffe-Maud Commission, 1969, p. 73).

The need to tackle planning problems in this way had already been illustrated in the field of transportation by the setting up from 1963 onwards of land-use transportation studies in each of the four major conurbations (West Midlands, Greater Manchester, Merseyside and Tyneside). In each case the Department of Transport (DoT) played a major role in bringing the various local authorities together to consider jointly the transportation problems of their areas, and to produce an investment plan to deal with them. The DoT achieved this partly through persuasion and partly through inducement (the studies were 50 per cent funded by the DoT) and insisted that each study employ consultants to produce an 'impartial, outsider's input' which is was hoped would override the more 'parochial' views and commitments of the constituent councils. (These views, of course, legitimately reflected the political programmes and mandates of such authorities.) The initiative may be seen as an attempt to create an (admittedly weak) conurbation – wide interest, to set against the many local interests in existence. The studies did subsequently result in plans, which were agreed (with one exception) by the constituent authorities, but at the cost of a certain amount of credibility, with highways networks being defined which have subsequently been recognized as quite excessive in relation to need. The problems and product of this process underlined the need for a single conurbation-wide planning authority. They also provided some useful insights into what might be expected of 'joint action' on planning and transportation after 1986, if the metropolitan counties are abolished. A further development in these areas was the setting-up in 1968 of conurbation-wide Transport Authorities in each of the four conurbations, prior to (though, it was argued, without prejudice to) the report of the Redcliffe-Maud Commission.

Although the emphasis differs in the two reports, with Herbert stressing the problems of inter-authority relations and Redcliffe-Maud the problems of economic and population growth, in each report the relationship between the increasing complexity of the environmental conditions is related to the inadequacy of the existing institutional arrangements to handle this complexity.

The Political and Organizational Dimensions

In both reorganizations, the influence of individual ministers was crucial in setting in motion the process of change. Present situation excepted, major reorganizations of local government require *inter alia* a strong commitment of the responsible minister. Without this, the forces of inertia in the existing system will invariably be too great (in this connection, the extremely slow progress of the Local Government (Boundary) Commission from 1958 to 1966 should be noted: see Wood, 1976, pp. 16 ff.).

In the case of London, it was Henry Brooke who first set things in motion by the appointment of the Herbert Commission, spurred on primarily by the intractability of the Middlesex problem (see above) and Sir Keith Joseph, who gave the process a new momentum when appointed as Minister of Housing and Local Government in 1962, just when it needed it (a general election was looming two years ahead). In the case of the provinces it was Richard Crossman, under pressure from his civil servants and experiencing increasing dissatisfaction with the cumbersome and ineffective machinery of the Local Government Commission, who in a relatively short period of time persuaded his Cabinet colleagues of the desirability of action (see Wood, 1976, pp. 17 ff.; Crossman, 1975, pp. 331 and *passim*).

In both cases also, the Royal Commissions set up were faced with a 'divided world' of local government, in an era when central government was much more concerned than it now is to keep on reasonably good terms with the major interests in that world, (for example, the local authority associations). The 1958–66 Local Government Commission had been set up with the agreement of the associations. In the case of Greater London, as Smallwood (1965, pp. 97 ff.) and G. Rhodes (1970, pp. 114 ff.) show, the major division was between the London County Council and the surrounding counties, whose basic position was to defend the status quo, and most of the district authorities, with the exception of those in Surrey and London. In Surrey the districts were equally divided for and against. In London the Labour-controlled London boroughs (with the significant exception of Fulham) continued to support the LCC's position. The local government associations, though they all gave evidence, played a fairly minor role in the proceedings, no doubt because the fate of the fringes of Greater London were of relatively marginal interest to them. The Herbert Commission, by producing a proposal which appealed to the majority of second-tier authorities in the fringe counties and subsequently to an increasing number of London boroughs, was able to generate a strong enough coalition of interest to push the proposal forward. The Conservative government of the time had clearly calculated that the break-up of the LCC, with its seemingly permanent Labour majority, was worth the (temporary?) alienation of predominantly Conservative-controlled fringe counties especially when the only other real casualty was Middlesex (which swung between Conservative and Labour control). Despite fierce opposition from the Labour Party, the Act setting up the new Greater London Council and the new boroughs reached the statute book months before the change of national government. Significantly, three major changes from the Herbert recommendation were made. First, the teaching lobby won a major concession in the continued existence of the old LCC area as an education authority (see G. Rhodes, 1970, pp. 186–9). Secondly, the area of the new Greater London authority was reduced, initially by some exclusions agreed by the Herbert Commission itself, and later and more predictably by the Conservative government which deleted from the new county significant chunks of the Surrey fringes of the Special Review Area. Thirdly, the powers of the new Greater London authority were diluted in that whereas the Herbert Commission recommended that the GLC should have responsibilities for education and housing policy and resource-allocation, education was subsequently made wholly the responsibility of the boroughs (outside the ILEA) and the GLC's housing powers were modified in such a way they became extremely difficult to apply effectively (see Young and Kramer, 1978). These changes reflected the normal processes of lobbying by affected interests, and in particular the ability of the predominantly Conservative-controlled district authorities outside the LCC area either to get themselves excluded altogether from the change, or to generate a shift in the balance of power from the new (and possibly Labour-controlled) GLC to the new (and probably predominantly Conservative-controlled) outer boroughs (see Smallwood, 1965, ch. 12). They have parallels in the modifications made to the Redcliffe-Maud proposals in the Local Government Act 1972, which were equally significant in the constraints they placed on the ability of the new metropolitan counties to fulfil their allotted roles.

In the case of the Redcliffe-Maud Commission, local government interests were also divided, with most small authorities (and the Association of Urban and Rural District Councils) indignant at the prospect of their future demise, or takeover by a larger adjacent authority. While some counties (for example, Cheshire) were equally concerned about their disappearance, others found themselves the basis of new unitary authorities with their boundaries barely disturbed and supported the proposals (see Wood, 1976, p. 76). Many county boroughs also gained – more unequivocally outside the proposed new metropolitan areas than within. In any event, the level of support – particularly amongst Labour-controlled authorities – was sufficient for the Labour government to produce a White Paper which set out to implement, with two important modifications (that is, two extra metropolitan counties to be set up in West Yorks and South Hants; the metropolitan counties also to be education and rating authorities), the recommendations of the Redcliffe-Maud Commission. These intentions were frustrated by the results of the 1970 general election. However as fate would have it, the incoming Conservative government and in particular Peter Walker with a manifesto commitment to the reform of the local government structure (and ironically to 'strengthen local government through a relaxation of central government controls'!) was happy to continue the momentum, if not the specific direction of change. Calculations of political advantage to the Conservative Party were clearly a major force in the modifications which were proposed in the 1971 White Paper to the previous 1969 Labour one. This point applies particularly to the curtailing of the boundaries of the new metropolitan counties (see Bristow *et al.*, 1984, p. 9). Indeed the boundaries were further curtailed as the Bill went through both Houses by some intensive and successful lobbying on the part both of small (and normally Conservative-controlled) districts such as Wilmslow which wished to avoid incorporation into the new metropolitan areas, and of the counties in which they were situated (see Wood, 1976, pp. 151–3). It applies also to the introduction of a further two new ones (Tyne and Wear and South Yorks, but minus South Hants); and the adoption of a two-tier system throughout the country, and not, as Redcliffe-Maud and the Labour White Paper proposed, just in the metropolitan areas. The switch of education from metropolitan county to metropolitan district level and the re-emergence of the metropolitan districts as rating authorities were also significant. The first reflected the strength of the dislike of the then Secretary of State for Education (Margaret Thatcher) of the ILEA, her determination to avoid the creation of 'another six ILEAS' and her ability so to persuade the Cabinet (Talk by Robin Pauley, 4 November 1983, to the RIPA/INLOGOV Conference on the Future of Metropolitan Government, published 1984). The second, which followed logically from the first (education is by far the biggest spending local government function) increased the psychological distance between the new metropolitan counties and the ratepayers/voters. Other changes, such as the introduction of highways agency and 'claiming' provisions for districts and the split of planning powers between county and district owed much to the strength of the lobby from the newly constituted district councils.

As with the Greater London Government Act, a sufficient coalition of support had been created notably and predictably from the existing (predominantly Conservative-controlled) counties (which survived the transition remarkably well), and with some exceptions, from the county boroughs which became the base of (usually extended) metropolitan districts. The main losers were the large county boroughs outside the metropolitan areas which became shire districts with considerably decreased status and power (for example, 'I weep for Nottingham', leader of the City Council – quoted in Wood, 1976, p. 110). As in the case of London, the changes from the purity of the Royal Commission's proposals, inspired predominantly by consideration of party political voting advantage, was to create numerous problems subsequently.

The *Organic Change* proposals, introduced by Peter Shore in 1979, although concerned primarily with the distribution of shire counties and shire districts, provide further evidence of the circumstances under which structural change does and does not take place. (A further example of abortive proposals for change – the move in the Conservative Party to abolish the Greater London Council in the mid-1970s – is discussed elsewhere: Chapter 3 below, and Young, 1984b.) Shore wished to return education and social services powers to the 'big nine' (the nine largest former county boroughs in the shire counties, for example, Nottingham, Bristol, Hull, Leicester), social services powers to an unspecified additional number of shire districts (the qualifying criteria were at least 100,000 population, an urban core, and preferably some previous experience of running the service: see Stewart *et al.*, 1979), and to make minor adjustments in favour of shire *and* metropolitan districts in the fields of planning and highways. The proposal was again inspired by consideration of party political advantage (most of the big nine were Labour controlled, while their counties were not), was not legitimized by the findings of any independent study or commission, did not generate a broad coalition of support, and ultimately did not survive the change in government in 1979. Indeed, even within the Labour government, the proposals were threatened by a strong rearguard action from the Secretaries of State for Education and the Social Services, and may not have carried (R. A. W. Rhodes *et al.*, 1982). There are some interesting parallels here with *Streamlining the Cities*. The proposed changes therein had not been recommended by any independent study or commission (indeed, the proposals have been widely criticized by the academic world – see SAUS, 1983; Raine, 1983; Greater London Group, 1984; Regional Studies Association, 1984), they had an extremely narrow base of support in the local government world, and were known not to be favoured by those members of the Cabinet with the most experience of local government (Talk by Pauley, 1984). The main difference in outcome may be in the size of the government's majority in the Commons and its ideology of resoluteness, epitomized by the commitment of the Prime Minister herself to the proposed changes (see ibid., 1984).

The Flawed Design of the GLC and the Metropolitan Counties

The task of the metropolitan counties (and the GLC) to establish themselves as bodies with a clear role and purpose was handicapped from the start by their design which was flawed in two major ways. First, their boundaries were unrealistic and in some cases their very *raison d'être* questionable; secondly, their powers were so limited and diluted (in comparison with the proposals of the Herbert and the Redcliffe-Maud Commissions) as to weaken considerably their coherence and comprehensibility as units of government. The doubts about their viability which have been regularly expressed since 1974 (and 1964) are the product of the political manoeuvring which modified the proposals of the Royal Commissions, as much if not more than their actual performance.

In the first place, it is doubtful whether some of the designated metropolitan counties cover areas which could justifiably be called metropoli, in the usual sense of the term (that is, a conglomeration of district communities which are bound together by their dependence upon the labour market and commercial opportunities afforded by a central city'). It is arguable whether West Yorkshire would qualify on this criterion, although there is a case on journey-pattern grounds for regarding it as a 'multi-nucleated' conurbation (see West Yorkshire PTE, 1984), and extremely doubtful whether South Yorkshire fits this conception. This reflects, of course, the changes in the 'shopping list' of metropolitan authorities between 1969 and 1972, from Redcliffe-Maud, to the Labour White Paper, to the 1972 Act. Of the four remaining 'viable' metropolitan counties, there are doubts about the inclusion of parts of their territory in each instance (Should Coventry be in West Midlands? Wigan in Greater Manchester? Southport in Merseyside? Sunderland associated with Tyneside?) and serious doubts about their boundaries generally (see below). Thus it is hard to defend the metropolitan counties as currently defined, as rational units of government.

With two exceptions (West and South Yorkshire – which are doubtful contenders for metropolitan status, but where the 'rural hinterland' is in each case quite considerable), it is widely argued that the metropolitan counties have been far too narrowly circumscribed in spatial terms (Wood, 1976, pp. 106, 186; Bristow *et al.*, 1984, p. 216). If 'continuous built-up area' and 'journey-to-work' patterns are taken as the main criteria, then as Redcliffe-Maud argued, much larger tracts of Lancashire and Cheshire should have been included in Merseyside and Greater Manchester. A similar argument applies to parts of Warwickshire, Worcestershire and Staffordshire in the West Midlands (where the boundaries are particularly tight) and to a lesser extent, parts of Durham and Northumberland in relation to Tyne and

Wear. It is a salutary exercise to compare Redcliffe-Maud's proposals for his three metropolitan counties with the boundaries which were subsequently designated in 1972. Even the truncated proposals of the 1971 White Paper were further trimmed by a number of famous (or notorious) last-minute escapes (for example, Wilmslow from Greater Manchester, Ellesmere Port from Merseyside) as the Bill passed through its various stages. It is, therefore, not surprising that the ability of the metropolitan counties to perform adequately their planning, and in some cases waste disposal functions, has been adversely affected by the nature of their boundaries.

Just as serious for the metropolitan counties' image and role were the changes between 1969 and 1972 in the functions which they were allocated. First, it is often forgotten that Redcliffe-Maud gave all land-use planning powers to the metropolitan counties (that is, structure planning, local planning and development control). Second, in the Labour Party's White Paper which followed Redcliffe-Maud's Report, education was also allocated to the metropolitan counties. What happened subsequently was that planning came to be divided very unsatisfactorily between metropolitan counties and metropolitan districts (see Chapter 4) and education was given (back) to the metropolitan districts (see p. 30 above). Third, the highways powers of metropolitan counties were significantly diluted both by the agency arrangements clause in the 1972 Act and the clause which enabled districts to claim the right to maintain unclassified roads. This had the effect of fragmenting the highways service in all but one of the metropolitan counties (West Yorks, where the county reached agreement with all districts, apart from Bradford, not to operate agency). Agency Arrangements for the construction and maintenance of highways and a range of other related highways functions were entered into by the metropolitan counties in 1973–4 partly because of shortage of staff (and under pressure from Circular 131/72, DoE, 1972), but also because of their awareness of the powers of the districts to 'claim' road maintenance of unclassified roads, if not offered an agency agreement. Claiming powers have in fact been used at various times since 1974 in Bradford, Birmingham and the four districts in South Yorks. These various machinations left the metropolitan counties without the exclusive and unified planning powers that Redcliffe-Maud had intended. They left them indeed with relatively few powers that were clearly and indisputedly their own; police – where real member involvement is difficult because of the Chief Constable's responsibility for all 'operational' matters; fire – which is relatively uncontentious politically anyway; trading standards, where the same point applies; waste disposal, which is another technically based service of low political salience (except in relation to site selection); and public transport, which has not surprisingly become in all the metropolitan counties the major area of political interest (except amongst Conservative candidates where it comes second to rates: see Bristow *et al.*, 1984, p. 82). With education lost, responsibility for highways blurred by agency, planning powers unsatisfactorily split up to 1980, and reduced considerably by the Local Government Planning and Land Act of that year, the argument that members of metropolitan counties have been 'looking for things to do' (see Calderwood, 1984) has some credibility. It is hardly conceivable that, had the metropolitan counties been given the functions which Redcliffe-Maud suggested plus education, their self-image, role and currently existence could be in such doubt. The metropolitan counties as created were counties without, in most cases, the boundaries to fit their planning and transportation functions or the functions suited to their boundaries. While the repercussions of these shortcomings were probably not recognized by the 1970–4 Conservative government (which put a lot of faith in the possibilities of county–district co-operation), the confusion in origin soon led inevitably to confusion in role and identity. B. Leach (1985) however argues that, although it is easy to blame the Conservative government of the time for effectively castrating the new metropolitan counties, at least some of the responsibility was the Redcliffe-Maud Commission's. Their insistence on the (arbitrary) top limit of a population of 1 million for running personal services is singled out as of particular significance.

The problem of confusion in origin of the Greater London Council was similar, though with some important differences. Again, there was considerable doubt as to whether its boundaries were drawn widely enough, with significant portions of disputed metropolitan fringe territory earmarked for inclusion by the Herbert Commission being withdrawn as the Bill passed through Parliament (see G. Rhodes, 1972, p. 195). There were doubts as in the metropolitan counties, whether the GLC had been given a range of functions which would give it a clear identity and role. Unlike the metropolitan counties, the GLC was given housing powers, though these were significantly whittled down between 1960 and 1963, and proved difficult to implement satisfactorily (see Young and Kramer, 1978) and education powers (indirectly) with regard to inner London. Like the metropolitan counties, the GLC has had to share land-use planning powers with the boroughs (the arrangements are somewhat different in Greater London than elsewhere, with the GLC having retained more development control powers than the metropolitan counties) and to share highways powers (London boroughs have certain highways powers as of right, unlike the metropolitan districts). Police has never been even nominally a GLC function, and even public transport has been controlled less directly (via London

Transport) than in the metropolitan areas. The GLC's functions have been watered down in other ways since 1964 (see Marshall, 1978, p. 6) and given its inadequate boundaries and unsatisfactory mix of functions, it is not surprising that similar doubts about its identity and role have been expressed over the years as those concerning the metropolitan counties (see Marshall, 1978, pp. 11–13).

The metropolitan authorities were conceived as planning authorities by the Royal Commission, when planning for an increased and increasing population was seen as the dominant purpose facing local authorities. The same was true by and large of Greater London. They have experienced a world in which population growth has reduced and planning has ceased to have that dominant focus. Indeed, most of the pressing problems identified by Redcliffe-Maud – housing overspill, pressure on green belts, competition for land, commuting problems, and so on – have if anything lessened rather than intensified over the years. The new metropolitan units, flawed in design, have been set in a changed world for which they were not designed.

That, however, does not necessarily mean that they do not have a role in an era of population stagnation or decline: Spence *et al.* (1983, p. 292) have argued:

> Britain is entering a phase of low to zero population growth. Planners are no longer concerned with the location of major new urban centres to meet the demands of an ever increasing population, but rather with careful propagation and resuscitation of some towns and certain parts of large cities. In such a no-growth situation it is of even greater importance to get the overall settlement strategy right. It is not so much that planning objectives have changed ... rather that the demographic and economic context has shifted.

What has perhaps become more apparent is that the planning role of metropolitan government should not be limited to land-use planning alone. The environmental pressures of the metropolis still exist, though less visibly than in an era of expansion. The problem is still to identify the most appropriate form of metropolitan government to deal with them (see Chapter 5).

The Politics of the Reform of Metropolitan Government

At a recent RIPA/INLOGOV conference, Ken Young argued that one of the problems with the GLC was that it was not powerful enough (in terms of its responsibilities) to be effective, but too powerful to be ignored (Young, 1984a, p. 5). This dilemma is equally true of the metropolitan counties. The problem of allocation of functions in a metropolitan area has always reflected in simple dualistic terms, the tension between its unity in the economic sphere, and its diversity in the social sphere. The economic unity creates a pressure towards a metropolitan-wide unit of government. The social diversity, particularly in relation to the difference in class structure between the inner metropolitan areas and suburbs (with their own self-image of 'separateness') results in political differentiation, and the pressure towards district or borough units based on areas which are (relatively) homogeneous, socially and politically. As Young puts it:

> We may regard the essential dualism of metropolitan life as a tension between the needs for area-wide administration of common services, and the forces for identity-maintaining suburban separatism.
>
> (Young, 1975, p. 135)

This tension has been addressed in different ways in different countries. In the USA, metropolitan reform proposals were considered seriously in the 1920s and 1930s and attempts made to rationalize city government, and to link needs and resources via metropolitan government. These attempts were almost universally defeated, mainly by suburban interests (see Young, 1984a, p. 7). In Europe although similar tensions are apparent, almost all countries are either moving towards the introduction, for the first time, of some form of metropolitan government, or are strengthening the metropolitan institutions which already exist (see Norton, 1983). What is clear is that whatever 'solution' is adopted, tensions between economic unity and social diversity do not disappear. There is no simple solution to the tension or dualism. In the past, the solutions advocated have varied between the 'weak metropolitanism' of, for example, the joint land-use transportation studies and planning exercises of the mid-1960s, which sought to generate voluntary agreement between the various independent authorities then existing, and the stronger metropolitanism of the Redcliffe-Maud proposals and, in particular, the Labour White Paper of 1969. The current arrangements, in both the GLC and the provinces may perhaps be classified as 'intermediate' – neither particularly strong nor weak – while the current government's proposals in *Streamlining the Cities* represent a reintroduction of an extremely weak form of metropolitanism (joint boards, joint committees, planning commissions and the like). The proposals do, however, implicitly acknowledge the need for some form of metropolitan government!

What is clear is that whatever set of governmental arrangements are applied to metropolitan areas, the underlying tension – between economic unity and social diversity – will remain (most strongly in Greater London, and least so in the 'doubtful' metropolis of West and South Yorkshire), and will in one way or another re-emerge. In the current two-tier system, the tensions emerge in the form of county–district conflicts. In a weaker form of metropolitanism, they would emerge as district–district or joint board–district tensions, with central government inevitably playing a greater mediating role. In a strong metropolitan system, the interests of certain areas (inner city versus the suburbs) and certain groups (the deprived versus the remainder) might be expected, in certain circumstances, to prevail, with no doubt rearguard actions on the part of those losing out, to get the system changed. Such conflicts of interest cannot be legislated away, although they can be stifled for a while, by a suitably confusing system of government.

In a sense what has happened is that the choice between 'strong' and 'weak' metropolitanism has been fudged in each of the recent reorganizations. The relatively strong role proposed for the GLC by Herbert was diluted into the 1963 legislation and has been further diluted since. The 'strong' metropolitanism of the Redcliffe-Maud proposals and the 1969 White Paper fell victim to the 1970–4 Conservative government's desire to preserve the shire counties and their preparedness to make concessions to district pressures. The current proposals, though undeniably involving a 'weak' form of metropolitanism are so confused and convoluted as to limit severely the possibility of any effective implementation of a metropolitan role. As with Layfield (see Stewart, 1983, p. 59) the real choice has been avoided, for all kinds of understandable political reasons. Strong metropolitan government has never had a fair chance in this country to demonstrate either its effectiveness (in strategic, planning or service delivery terms) or its long-term acceptability. Neither has any government since the 1960s been prepared totally to ignore the need for that role, or take it on itself.

The Different Roles of Metropolitan County Councils

In the light of the modifications made to the Royal Commission's proposals for Greater London and the provincial metropoli and the lack of clarity surrounding their eventual allocation of functions, it is important to clarify what roles it is that the GLC and the MCCs are supposed to be playing and to compare these with other possible role configurations.

The most comprehensive list of possible roles for a metropolitan authority is to be found in the report of the Marshall Inquiry on Greater London (1978). This lists seven possible roles for a metropolitan authority (wider functional; specialist; co-ordinating; strategic/planning; strategic/executive; corporate planning; and strategic/directory: ibid., p. 12). Inherent in these distinctions are three different broader conceptions of metropolitan roles.

(i) A functional role

This would embrace Marshall's 'wider functional' and 'specialist' categories. The argument involved is a familiar one – that certain services can be much more effectively or efficiently carried out at a spatial scale wider than that of the lower-tier authority. Services customarily cited in this connection include fire, police, waste disposal and public transport. There are two important riders to this argument – first, that the most appropriate size (population or geographical) for any particular service is and always has been open to a wide variety of different interpretations and views: and secondly, that even if it is accepted that a metropolitan scale for some particular function or service is the most appropriate, this does not of itself imply a unit of metropolitan government. This qualification would apply particularly to several of the services cited in Marshall's second (specialist) role, for example, intelligence, computer services, historic buildings, and so on, where the political salience of the activity is low.

(ii) A strategic role

This would embrace Marshall's categories of 'co-ordination', 'strategic/planning' and 'strategic/executive', taking the concept of 'strategy' as 'an appropriate response to a policy problem which involves the complex interaction of a number of distinct elements which are interrelated in such a way that the treatment of the elements in isolation from one another may be insufficient to cope with the problem'. On this basis, 'co-ordination' may be seen as a 'weak' strategic role, strategic/planning as an intermediate one and strategic/executive as a 'strong' variant. The main issue of concern here is for what particular interrelated set of elements is a strategy an appropriate response, at the metropolitan level. The main elements have typically involved some combination of land-use planning, transportation, servicing and (latterly) economic development responsibilities.

(iii) A resource-allocation role

This would cover Marshall's 'corporate planning' and 'strategic/ directing' categories. In a sense we are also talking about a strategic role here, but one which is so different in conception from the one discussed above that it is worth considering separately. The distinctive elements would be (1) a wider range of functions (compared with the more limited 'land-use/transportation' nexus normally associated with the strategic role; (2) a clear hierarchy of power with the metropolitan authority providing and being able to enforce an overall framework within which the lower-tier and other public authorities have to work; and (3) a resource-allocation element which would involve the transfer of responsibilities currently carried out by central government – rate support grant (RSG), capital allocations – to the metropolitan authority. It would involve the metropolitan authority in the distribution of finance to the second–tier authorities on the basis of their assessment of the district's needs.

Marshall reported in 1978 when the GLC was Conservative controlled and before the programme of the new left was apparent, let alone in the process of being implemented. It was perhaps not surprising therefore that a fourth role for metropolitan authorities – an interventionist role – was not considered in his report. The term, however, does seem the most appropriate way of labelling a range of activities pursued since 1981 by the GLC and, to a lesser extent, by the MCCs. This role stresses the duty of a local authority to develop a policy stance on a wide range of topical issues which are manifested within (and indeed sometimes outside) its boundaries, and to use whatever opportunities are available to implement such policy stances. Employment creation, equal opportunities (race and sex) civil defence and even (in the case of the GLC) the situation in Northern Ireland, have been some of the major issues concerned. This role implies a wide, almost all-embracing view of the responsibilities of local government. It combines the notion that a local authority has a legitimate interest in everything within its area, with the view that the local authority has a duty to act as 'superior spokesman' for the area. This concept of localism/nationalism has involved an unwelcome challenge to central government both in principle, and over several particular issues normally regarded as the exclusive province of the latter.

Elements of each of these roles can be identified in the current activities of the GLC and the MCCs. There are for example a number of services which MCCs and the GLC carry out because it was judged that such services could be more appropriately run on a metropolitan-wide basis, as opposed to a sub-metropolitan scale. 'Economies of scale', metropolitan-wide nature of the problem, and 'need for specialist expertise which the districts individually could not justify' were the major arguments used. Into this category came police, fire, public transport, trading standards (including consumer protection) and in some cases provision for the arts (museums, art galleries, theatres). A distinction should be made between functions allocated to MCCs on an economies of scale basis (for example, fire, public transport) and those so allocated because of a desire for uniform standards (for example, trading standards, consumer protection).

There are other functions which are carried out at metropolitan level because the interrelated problems they address are of a level of complexity (see definition on p. 38 above) such as to require a strategic approach on a metropolitan-wide scale. These are the traditional strategic functions and comprise the linked topics of land-use planning and transportation planning together with certain aspects of economic development and housing. There is no implication that the current powers available to the GLC and MCCs under these headings are adequate to enable them to carry out their strategic role effectively.

The resource-allocation role is found only in embryo form, in the process of allocation of resources by the metropolitan counties (and the GLC) to the districts (and boroughs) to carry out highway construction, maintenance and other associated activities under highways agency agreements. Here the county assesses the standard of highway conditions across the county, on a consistent basis, using some kind of objective measure, and then allocates resources to the districts to carry out the work. The basis of this allocation (in principle at any rate) on the maintenance side, is the equalization of highway conditions across the county. In practice, the resource allocation implications of the results of the survey have usually been scaled down, because they would have produced too great a discrepancy from previous patterns of expenditure if applied rigorously. It could also be argued that the provision of grants to firms by MCC-sponsored enterprise boards and of grants to voluntary groups of various kinds provide a further example of the same process of resource allocation, although criteria different from that of 'equalization of standard' may apply in these cases (for example, positive discrimination in favour of areas of greater need). There already exists, of course, one kind of equalization process in London – the rate equalization scheme. This is, however, administered by the DoE in consultation with the London boroughs.

A 'resource-allocation' role for the GLC was argued for strongly by the Director-General's Board in their evidence to the Marshall Inquiry and he was clearly convinced by their arguments by the time he came to write his report. He recommended 'the assumption by the strategic authority of central government's role for the allocation within Greater London of global sums determined by Whitehall'. Within this constraint, the GLC would have powers over the authorization of capital and other long-term financial developments over a range of London's public services, adequate and independent forms of local taxation and the distribution of Exchequer grant within London, including not just RSG but a range of other special grants (Marshall, 1978, p. 100). This role is also advocated by the Association of London Authorities and the current GLC leadership. A number of different criteria could, of course, be used to distribute the grants. A Labour-controlled MCC would no doubt be concerned to use such grants redistributively to benefit those areas (and boroughs) in the greatest social need (as the current GLC does in its grants to voluntary bodies). A Conservative-controlled MCC would perhaps be more concerned with criteria such as 'previous patterns of expenditure' or 'equal expenditure per head of population'. In principle the same arguments could be used to advocate a 'resource-allocation' role for the metropolitan counties. In practice, it is hard to conceive of any central government giving up such powers to any kind of local authority. Certainly that particular recommendation of Marshall's (as many others) fell on stony ground.

The fourth role – the interventionist role – is the role which it seems likely that the government have in mind when referring to 'the search for a wider role . . . which may lead them to promote policies which conflict with national policies which are the responsibility of central government' (DoE, 1983, para. 1.12). Its main areas of application have already been noted. It is of particular significance in a consideration of the recent history of the GLC (see Chapter 3).

Table 2.1 *MCC/GLC functions: a role categorization*

	Wider functional	Strategic	Resource allocation	Interventionalist
Police	**		*	*(GLC)
Fire	**		*	
Waste disposal	**		*	
Trading standards & consumer protection	**			
Land-use planning		**		
Public transport	**	**	*	
Highways	*	**	**	
Economic development		*	*	**
Arts & recreation	*		*	
Equal opportunities			*	*
N. Ireland, Civil Defence, etc				**

** Primary Role
* Secondary Role

This role categorization does not enable each function which is or could be carried out by MCCs or the GLC to be allocated exclusively to one category or the other (see Table 2.1). Clearly there are overlaps. Some functions (for example, public transport) have an element of both 'strategic' and 'wider functional' roles. Functions such as fire and waste disposal have a resource-allocation dimension, with the MCCs themselves distributing resources in such a way that some areas within their territory are bound to benefit more than others. Functions labelled as 'interventionist' may also be 'strategic' if dealt with in a 'strategic' fashion and linked to other functions of strategic concern. However, the classification does help to clarify what has become a very muddy debate about the supposedly 'strategic' role of the GLC and the MCCs.

Thus in assessing the performance of the MCCs and the GLC and in evaluating the likely effect of the proposed alternative arrangements, these distinctions should be borne in mind. Could the district – either individually or collectively – carry out the 'service-delivery' functions of the metropolitan counties as efficiently and effectively; or would economies of scale inevitably be lost? Could the districts – either individually or collectively – carry out the strategic functions currently undertaken by the metropolitan counties in any meaningful sense? Who would perform the (admittedly limited) resource allocation role currently undertaken by the metropolitan counties? And is there a case for an 'interventionist' local authority at the metropolitan level, in what we are frequently reminded is a unitary state? The implications of the government's proposals would seem to be that the interventionist role is not regarded as a legitimate one; that the limited amount of resource allocation currently carried out by the GLC and the MCCs should be carried out by the DoE and DoT; that the wider functional role should be carried out by the boroughs or districts acting jointly or by the proposed joint boards; and that the strategic role should be carried out partly again by inter-borough co-operation but mainly through increased involvement by the DoE and DoT.

The Current Confusion over the roles of the GLC and the Metropolitan County Councils

In the series of debates that have taken place about the need for some form of 'metropolitan' or 'city regional' government since the Second World War, it is the strategic role which has featured most prominently. Although the concept of a strategic role did not come to be used explicitly until after the publication of the Report of the Herbert Commission, its component elements had been discussed and advocated for some time previously. The physical growth of the major cities in the 1920s and 1930s, fuelled by the development of motor transport, and the impact of war damage (with its implied need/opportunity for new radical solutions) were key factors here. A conviction grew that such areas should ideally be planned as a whole, that the complex interrelationship of different activities in metropolitan areas required more than mere co-ordination (see for example, Abercrombie, 1945). The major problems which were seen as necessitating this kind of strategic planning were the interrelationship between land-use patterns and transportation; the problems of the redistribution of population and housing and employment opportunities within metropolitan areas; the awareness of the externalities of major developments such as shopping centres and offices in one part of the metropolitan area, on other parts; and more recently the particular problems of inner city deprivation. Thus the concept of strategy which has informed the various debates about metropolitan functions, has been firmly grounded in the language and perspective of land-use planning. There are of course other more wide-ranging and ambitious conceptions of strategic planning (see for example Eversley, 1984, p. 14). In the event as Eversley shows, it has proved difficult for the GLC (and indeed the MCCs) to fulfil their (limited) strategic planning role effectively in the light of the increasing tendency for central government to intervene over major decisions. The government's view in the White Paper was that strategic planning should be regarded as a 'passing fashion' (para. 1.3), although it is in fact safeguarded as an activity in the more detailed proposals (see Chapter 1). The major 'wider functional' services were, as B. Leach (1985) shows, 'tacked on' to the MCCs' responsibilities by Redcliffe-Maud, and subsequently by the 1970–4 Conservative government. They were in no sense the *raison d'être* of the MCCs. They were allocated to the MCCs because the existence of the MCCs was deemed to be necessary on strategic planning grounds, and police, fire and waste disposal, unlike social services and education, were not the kind of services which Redcliffe-Maud felt had to be handled, for accessibility reasons, at the lower-tier level.

The White Paper on *Streamlining the City* dismissed the strategic role of the metropolitan counties and the GLC.

In this situation the GLC and MCCs have found it difficult to establish a role for themselves. Most of the real power rests with the Borough and District Councils. The upper-tier authorities have a large rate-base, and an apparently wider remit. This generates a natural search for a 'strategic' role which may have little basis in real needs. What is more, in most policy areas, the implementation of such strategic views as may be developed depends, on practice, on the agreement of the Borough or District Councils which may not be forthcoming.

(DoE, 1983)

The White Paper records the view of the government both that the MCCs have failed to establish a strategic role or indeed that such a role is required, but does not give an adequate account of why previous Conservative governments sought to set up such authorities. One can barely understand from the White Paper how such a decision was ever arrived at. The MCCs in their response to the White Paper reassert the case for a strategic authority:

The government attempts to devalue the strategic countrywide arrangements for more than 80% of MCC current expenditure. The government ignores the body of evidence from objective studies that reiterates the need for the interrelated problems of the major conurbations to be handled in a comprehensive and strategic manner.

(Metropolitan Counties, 1984)

It could be argued that both the MCCs and the government are confused in their treatment of the strategic role of the county council. The MCCs appear to be equating 'strategic' with 'countywide' but the argument that it is desirable to have a particular function exercised at county level on efficiency grounds does not make it necessarily a strategic function. To use the word 'strategic' in this way robs the word of any distinctive meaning.

Indeed, three points about the relationship between a strategic role and strategic authorities should be stressed. First, problems or groups of problems for which strategies are seen to be required do not necessarily involve authorities currently deemed to be strategic (for example, 'housing' strategies in Housing Investment Programmes, HIPs). Secondly, strategic problems of a broader spatial scale, such as planning/transportation in a conurbation or region, have not always been viewed as implying the need for separate strategic authorities (for example, the various regional studies/plans of the 1960s and 1970s). Thirdly, the responsibilities of current strategic authorities quite clearly do not all relate to genuine strategic problems.

Thus to speak of MCCs – or any other unit of local government for that matter – as a strategic authority can be misleading because it can suggest *either* that such an authority deals only with strategic questions *or* that other types of authorities do not deal with strategic questions *or* both. Neither proposition is, of course, true of MCCs. Furthermore to suggest that a metropolitan county is a strategic authority can lead to a number of untenable views. First, it could imply that a function should be given to the metropolitan county because it is a strategic function. This would not be valid if the strategic function in question could realistically be carried out within the area of a metropolitan district (that is, if it was not necessarily associated with large-scale areas). Secondly, it could imply that because a function is carried out by a metropolitan county it is strategic in nature. It may be carried out by this type of authority because of alleged economies of scale, because of the scarcity of particular resources at district level, or merely because historically it has been carried out at metropolitan level. Thirdly, it could imply that 'urban strategy' is concerned with the functions that happen to be carried out by the strategic authority. This would and indeed, in many commentators' view, has led to the danger of interpreting urban strategy solely in physical or transportation terms. Urban strategy is not necessarily to be equated with land-use planning strategy. The identification of these two factors has encouraged the confusion between the strategic role and the metropolitan role. If the definition of strategy given earlier is accepted, then it has to be recognized that many lower-tier authorities deal with complex, intractable and interrelated problems. Geographical scale and strategic do not necessarily coincide. It may well be, however, that for certain issues, strategic does imply scale.

By presenting the issue in this way, a number of points become clearer. Both metropolitan authorities and district authorities have strategic and non-strategic functions. Functions were not allocated to the metropolitan county because they were strategic but because they required a larger area (though they may also be strategic). Thus it is not particularly helpful in clarifying the argument, either to describe the metropolitan county as a strategic authority or to use 'strategic' as a criterion for the allocation of functions to the county.

Having acknowledged this, the disadvantages of not having to separate authority to tackle those problems which stem from the economic unity of our major conurbations should be underlined. The political and other weaknesses of joint operations have been well-documented (see Flynn and Leach, 1984). The government view of strategic planning as a passing fad should be recognized for what it is: an argument of convenience. The complex interrelationships between economic development, housing opportunity, land-use and transportation, particularly in Greater London, have not disappeared since the 1960s. They have perhaps resulted in fewer 'big issues' (for example, housing overspill, motorway boxes, and so on) because of the depressed level of economic activity and population growth. However, ironically, as soon as the long-awaited economic upturn occurs, the incidence of major 'strategic issues' will soon become apparent!

3   The GLC: Two Decades of Experience

One would have thought that the proposition that Londoners should have an effective say in shaping their environment would have an obvious appeal. Those who find it unpalatable must face up to the question of what they would have instead.

(Sir Keith Joseph moving the second reading of the Bill to establish the GLC, 1962)

The towns around London have no meaning and no reason for existence except in relation to London; and many of the problems of metropolitan administration at the present time are directly due to the fact that they are arbitrarily cut off from London by municipal and county boundaries, without any wider form of common organisation to bring them together into a single unit.

(G. D. H. Cole, *The Future of Local Government*, Cassell, 1921)

Viewing London Differently

London has a unique system of local government. In part this reflects the exceptional character of the London region. Geographically it is not the largest metropolitan area, but its intense urbanization gives it a population more than two and a half times its nearest rival, the West Midlands. The GLC provides services to a population greater than that of several European nations; to one in eight Britons. London is the nation's capital and a world centre of business, finance, culture and tourism. Its rate base is huge; more than four times that of the West Midlands or Greater Manchester. London's needs and problems are those of the great cities of the Western world – Paris, New York, Rome, Tokyo. What, must be asked, has it in common with the wool towns of Yorkshire or the industrial villages of the Black Country?

Part of the history of administrative arrangements in London has been two-tier local government. Outside London the system which endured from the nineteenth century to the 1974 reorganization established single-tier county borough government in every main urban centre. The London Government Act 1899 created a system of metropolitan boroughs to work beneath the earlier created London County Council (LCC), thus establishing two-tier government over roughly the area of present-day inner London.

Behind such arrangements was the assumption that a special system of local government was required in London to meet the city's special needs. Differences have been compounded by the practice of undertaking reform in London and the provinces at different times and making separate legislation for London.

The 1983 White Paper breaks with these traditions. While recognizing that reform must take account of existing differences, it nowhere takes as axiomatic the notion that London requires a special form of metropolitan government. Such a position runs counter to the frameworks used by academics and practitioners to view local government and to a century of tradition and practice. It raises key questions for both abolition and reform to which this chapter returns later.

The Coming of the GLC

The late 1950s and early 1960s left their mark on the GLC when it came into being in 1964. It was a period of prosperity and growth when big was still considered potentially beautiful; and the GLC was big in every way. A borough planning officer, comparing the GLC to its predecessor the LCC, once remarked that it was twice as big, took twice as long, at twice the cost with twice the number of people. An untrue statement perhaps, but a popular perception.

The initiative for reform had come from central government, the ideas from professionals and academics. The existing local authorities and local politicians had overwhelmingly defended the status quo. The GLC was from birth a compromise. Labour had been placated by the retention of much of the old LCC in the work of the new GLC and the exclusion of many outer Conservative suburbs. The physical limitation of London had pleased the Conservatives fearful of a mass movement of population outwards; they had been pleased by the limitations placed upon the GLC's powers of strategic intervention and service provision, particularly in housing and planning.

The GLC was also an experiment. Its inception was the first major reform of metropolitan government in modern times. It not only extended two-tier government across an entire conurbation, but also developed the notion of a two-tier government as strategic and non-strategic government. Thus the GLC was given tasks which were thought to require city-wide administration for a variety of reasons. The GLC was in this way given a variety of roles – service provider, strategic planning authority, resource allocator – none of which was drawn up very coherently or with concern for the possible incompatibility of such varied activities.

The present authority differs from the GLC established in the London Government Act 1963. New legislation has given it new duties and taken away others. The social and economic environment has changed and so too have the needs and problems of London. Changes in the political climate have given rise to new priorities and programmes as well as new conflicts and alliances. Over two decades the weaker assumptions and less satisfactory provisions of the 1963 Act have been tested many times over, and the system forced to adjust.

Who does what in London Local Government

Local government in London provides broadly the same set of services as local authorities in other parts of the country. There are two key exceptions. The GLC has no responsibility for the police; the Metropolitan Police are the responsibility of the Home Secretary on the grounds that they provide many special services of national importance. The second exception concerns transport. London Transport never had the power to provide rail services in conjunction with British Rail and its huge commuting networks, which were open to other Passenger Transport Executives. Furthermore in June 1984 public transport was removed altogether from the hands of the GLC and given to a special agency appointed by central government, London Regional Transport.

The other key distinction between London local government and that in the other metropolitan areas lies in the way responsibilities are shared between the two layers. Turning first to the upper level, we find the GLC involved in areas closed to metropolitan counties. All bear the imprint of the old LCC. In the first place, the GLC is a housing authority in its own right possessing broadly the same powers as a borough. The allocation of such powers reflects not only political compromise but also the very real doubts of the ability of a set of boroughs to solve London's housing problems each within its own boundaries. There have been, however, considerable legal and political constraints upon the use of the GLC's housing powers (Young and Kramer, 1978) and the GLC's housing role has been in recent years in steep decline, particularly following the 1980 transfers of GLC housing stock to the boroughs. The ability and desire of the GLC to perform a key housing role in London is essential to an understanding of the performance of the capital's local government system.

Secondly, the GLC is, indirectly through the Inner London Education Authority (ILEA), an education authority for part of London. ILEA, which provides a comprehensive education service to thirteen inner London boroughs, is a special committee of the GLC and is supported administratively by the GLC. It is the direct descendant of the LCC education department and, as the country's largest education authority, has steadfastly resisted two attempts to abolish it in recent years. It operates in an area of London where need is high, resources very unevenly distributed, and several of the boroughs fall well below the size considered appropriate for a modern education service.

Thirdly, the GLC retains a detailed involvement in planning which was removed from the MCCs by the Local Government Planning and Land Act 1980. A small number of extremely significant planning applications have to be referred by the boroughs to the GLC. Given the growing obsolescence of the capital's structure plan, the Greater London Development Plan, the GLC is able to pursue new planning strategies through the development control process.

The boroughs also have responsibilities which their metropolitan counterparts lack. They are responsible for consumer protection. The boroughs also play a different role in the transport field. In London the highway network is divided into trunk roads (the responsibility of the Department of Transport), metropolitan roads (the responsibility of the GLC) and non-metropolitan roads (the responsibility of the boroughs). Boroughs play a considerable role in highway provision acting frequently as agents for the GLC and DoT.

As in the metropolitan counties it is the lower tier, the boroughs, which are clearly the primary units of local government. The GLC spends less than a fifth of all local government expenditure in London – see the figures in Appendix 2. The costliest services provided by the GLC in terms of recurrent expenditure have been public transport and housing, accounting for more than twice the authority's other programmes put together.

The GLC is a wide-ranging authority. The logic of the roles it has developed, however, is hard to discern. In terms of the four strategic roles for metropolitan authorities described in Chapter 2, the GLC can be seen at times to perform all four. As a service provider it has partial responsibility for the emergency and protective services; an interest in housing and education (though not in the personal social services); it has a role to play in leisure, and in transport. The GLC is a strategic planning authority through its role in land-use planning, transportation and, to a limited extent, housing. The GLC can, and has, intervened in a number of aspects of London's life in ways which it considers strategic. This has been possible under the several powers possessed by all local authorities. The areas the GLC has chosen to intervene in most recently have included economic development, the police, Northern Ireland and the conditions of women and minorities. Some of this has involved the provision of new services, some of it the extension of grant-giving to particular groups and those concerned with their activities and welfare. The fourth role open to strategic authorities identified by Marshall and promoted by the present GLC as a field for development is that of allocator of resources to other local authorities. At present this is limited to the financing of highways agency agreements with the boroughs, residual financial responsibilities towards transferred housing stock, and 'topping-up' of expenditure in certain boroughs on projects identified as compatible with GLC spending priorities. The effectiveness of the GLC in performing such roles is discussed further in considering the council's response to key issues in the London area.

The GLC and the Boroughs

It is seldom realized how much interaction there is between the tiers of local government. The division of responsibility between the GLC and the boroughs requires them to interact in a number of ways; in addition they may choose to co-operate voluntarily. The existence of the GLC is often taken for granted by boroughs on workaday matters and remembered only on more controversial points. The two layers of government in London are knit together in a way which makes prising them apart no easy matter.

The relationship between the GLC and the boroughs is central to the case put forward in the White Paper because of its alleged unsatisfactory nature. What is this relationship which has apparently failed? The relationship varies across services, which can be divided into three groups. In the first group we find planning and transport matters where both levels have a substantial involvement and they are obliged to a greater or lesser extent to work together. The GLC is the strategic planning authority; the boroughs the development control authorities. As mentioned above the boroughs must refer certain decisions to the GLC. Both levels are obliged by statute to consult each other on a great range of planning matters. The GLC also provides specialist services to the boroughs, most notably through the Historic Buildings Division. Not only the professionals but also the politicians must interact, since referred decisions go through the committee system of both authorities.

Transport is the other field where interaction is generally substantial. Boroughs undertake highway construction and maintenance and street lighting as agents of the GLC, who purchase borough engineering services from design to implementation. A further aspect of the relationship stems from the fact that the GLC is responsible for all traffic management on all London's non-trunk roads. Traffic problems are felt at the local level and boroughs have to apply to the GLC for the installation of traffic measures and provisions for pedestrians such as zebra crossings. Both professionals and members are involved in such schemes.

The second group of services are those where interaction is necessitated on specific aspects, namely finance, housing and the environment. Like all metropolitan district councils the boroughs set and collect a rate upon which the GLC precepts. This gives rise to an extremely formal relationship whereby the boroughs are requested to collect and remit moneys. There is no notion of joint financial planning involved and limited concern by the GLC for the impact of its budget on the boroughs. Interaction on housing centres on the stock handed over by the GLC, some of it in the early 1970s, the majority in 1980. The boroughs manage the property with their own stock but the GLC is obliged to fulfil certain conditions on renovating and modernizing the properties. Boroughs must also contribute a percentage of the vacancies in their acquired stock to a mobility scheme run by the GLC. Housing is no longer the area of stormy inter-tier relationships that it was in the past but more an area where junior and middle-ranking housing officers liaise on details of renovation programmes, and assistants input the details of would-be mobile tenants on to computer terminals.

In the field of the environment the two tiers must interact over rubbish. Boroughs collect it and the GLC disposes of it. At times it is a tricky operation: few people welcome rubbish, least of all that from other areas. The finer details of the operation of collecting systems impinge on an area of sensitive employee relations. The GLC and the boroughs also find themselves involved differently, one as licensing authority, one as planning authority, with respect to private tips.

In the other areas of local government service provision, there is little or no necessity for the two levels to interact, and so little interaction takes place. Both tiers provide leisure facilities but there is no joint plan or strategy. Each is responsible for education in a particular sector of London and interaction amounts to remitting fees to cross-border students and circulating information. The GLC's fire service inspects borough residential homes for fire safety, and residents in such homes may consume meals and sit on chairs purchased from the GLC's supplies service. In all other respects the fire service, personal social services and management services are the affairs of particular authorities. Both tiers can and do attempt to foster industry and employment but there is no joint planning and few joint projects.

The generally clear separation of the services between the GLC and the boroughs masks the extent of their interdependence. The division between the tiers cuts across groups of linked services and provides a considerable potential for interaction. In some authorities that potential is realized far more than others, hence the considerable variation which can be found between boroughs.

Boroughs vary in their relationship with the GLC along three main dimensions. First, there is obviously a difference between inner and outer London because of the existence of ILEA. Secondly, certain areas give rise to certain problems which affect the way the two tiers work together. For example, the vast LCC and GLC housing estates in Tower Hamlets could not simply be transferred to the borough and have given rise to a complicated and controversial act of joint management arrangements. The GLC worked closely with those boroughs liable to flood prior to the opening in 1984 of the Thames Barrier.

By far the major determinant of any pattern in the relationships between the tiers is politics. Conservative administrations work with Labour ones and with any other groupings that may emerge. Political rhetoric may be colourful but beneath this level professionals carry on business as usual between authorities of a different complexion. However, where both levels are of the same persuasion (not merely the same party, but the same ideological faction of that party) relationships can become more informal, politicians are in closer touch, and there is mutual interest in working together beyond the requirements of the law and good administration. Ken Livingstone's administration in County Hall has fostered a lot of voluntary joint action over the entire range of local government services with a number of Labour boroughs with like-minded politicians. Conversely it has found itself with some spectacularly unproductive relationships with certain right-wing Conservative boroughs.

The pattern of relationships between the boroughs and the GLC has changed over time apart from change precipitated by the ballot box. The boroughs have become more confident and independent-minded over two decades. The GLC has gradually moved away from its LCC image and role and become more open and outward looking. But memories are long in local government: politicians and officers still talk nostalgically of the days of Middlesex and the LCC. After two decades the two-tier system in London has not been totally accepted or its problems adequately solved in the minds of many.

Collective Intermediaries

One of the key differences between London and the other metropolitan areas is the number of lower-tier units in the system:

thirty-three. Inevitably the GLC has to adopt a more standardized approach to the boroughs, and the boroughs in their turn have found it necessary to act collectively towards government and the GLC.

Before reorganization a Metropolitan Boroughs Committee operated in London from which the London Boroughs Association (LBA) evolved. The London Government Act 1963 gave the LBA a statutory role in a number of areas as a body which 'appears to the Secretary of State to be representative'. Private legislation such as the GLC General Powers Acts has increased that role. Areas of activity include assistance to voluntary associations, currently about £0·5 million per annum, which is collected from all the boroughs at an agreed rate and disbursed through the GLC.

The LBA is not primarily executive. Its roles are those of an advocate and intermediary and adviser to its constituent members. Here its structure and mode of operation become crucial. Member authorities each send three members to the full association and one to each of its main committees, generally the key figures and chairmen from the boroughs. Committees are backed by officers' groups headed by Chief Officers from the boroughs. The politics of the LBA reflect the politics of the boroughs. As a voluntary association it must work by consensus and partisanship clearly places limits upon the issues it can tackle.

The current proposals have turned a spotlight onto the LBA. That light has fallen from two quite different directions. On the one hand the proposal to abolish the GLC has raised a suggestion which many Conservative boroughs have nurtured for a long time, that the LBA assume the role of co-ordinator of any activity requiring cross-borough action. Critics point to the political weakness of the LBA and its non-executive basis. None the less it remains one of the most popular candidates to succeed part of the GLC's role. On the other hand, some Labour boroughs unhappy with the LBA's Conservative priorities and its inability to adopt radical strategies have broken away from the LBA and formed a rival organization, the Association of London Authorities (ALA). The GLC was instrumental in setting up the ALA, which comprises a group of like-minded Labour boroughs, but was prevented by the courts from becoming a paying member. The split has polarized the boroughs and turned the LBA primarily into a mouthpiece for the Conservative boroughs, thus undermining its primary role as a London-wide forum.

The LBA and now the ALA are the local equivalent of the local authority associations, though more the creatures of their constituent members (Isaac-Henry, 1984). London is also criss-crossed by numerous professional and political networks embracing both tiers of government which make coherent government possible in a fragmented system. In London there was no 1974 reorganization to distribute staff and members among the new authorities. The GLC has always operated its own staffing structures, rather like a mini civil service and staff interchange between the tiers has been low. Such networks are vital in holding the system together in view of the often distant and at times deliberately cool relationships that have existed between the GLC and the boroughs.

Relationships with Central Government

As the nation's capital London enjoys a peculiar relationship with central government. Every MP works in London and has an opinion on the services provided by London's local government. The GLC has accounted for a large and growing element in total local government expenditure and disproportionate amounts of certain types of expenditure such as nearly a quarter of the Transport Supplementary Grant. Since Ken Livingstone took office the GLC has been one of a number of Labour local authorities which has openly challenged central government's social and economic policy both in word and deed. London's sheer size makes it a more significant challenge. Furthermore, opposition by Labour local authorities, notably the GLC, has spearheaded nation-wide opposition to Conservative policies, taking the initiative from the parliamentary Opposition (Boddy and Fudge, 1984).

Many critics have seen plans to abolish the GLC in terms of personal antipathy between Margaret Thatcher and Ken Livingstone. Clearly there is much more to the antagonism than that. By virtue of its size and gigantic rate base the GLC has been able to defy spending controls and penalties. (The GLC for several years received no rate support grant because of its 'overspending'.) Flamboyant leadership and radical initiatives have ensured it a wide and critical press which it has turned very successfully to its own advantage. How lasting and significant the challenge it poses is hard to assess. Certainly the GLC has goaded central government in a way that no other local authority has done in recent times. Ken Livingstone's view, expressed in an interview with the authors, is that Westminster sees the GLC as 'a giant pile of dog-mess on the other side of the river which it has a duty to clean up'.

London's Political Profile

London, like all the metropolitan areas, combines elements of extreme political stability with patterns of extreme instability. This pattern is illustrated in Figure 3.1. Since its inception political control of the GLC has swung back and forth in time neither with the boroughs nor with central government. Political congruence between the three levels has existed in four periods covering less than half the system's history with Labour enjoying six years of such dominance compared with the Conservative's three years. Such patterns underly the present government's frustration with the system: as soon as they get hold of part of it, another piece slips from their grasp. The frustration is compounded by the fixed terms of office of local authorities which make it impossible to 'time' elections.

London also has certain political characteristics which pertain to a far lesser extent in the other metropolitan areas. The boroughs cover the full political spectrum from the right of the Conservative Party to the left of the Labour Party. Following defeats in the 1968 borough elections, a younger, more radical and very committed set of Labour politicians swept through London Labour parties. The fortunes of such factions have ebbed and flowed over the years, but it is that group and their successors which have been making political waves in London in recent years. The smallness and homogeneity of many London boroughs guarantee an existence for both the left and the right in London politics regardless of the overall swings of power. It was the successors to 1968 who took power in the GLC immediately following the May 1981 Labour victory in the GLC elections: they had never captured so prized a platform before. With a right-wing Conservative government firmly entrenched in Westminster and a Conservative-dominated second tier elected as the Labour government's unpopularity started to climb (both centre and boroughs were to become stronger Conservative bastions in elections following the Falklands War) the scene was set for the most explosive set of relationships since the GLC was established. Never before had the two-party sandwich lined up in this way for any appreciable length of time nor had the ideologies of the parties ever been so different. In addition, both parties were being rattled by the SDP–Liberal Alliance in certain localities.

A unique feature of London politics which bears upon the question of abolition or reform is that the existence of the GLC has itself been an election issue and a focus of political organization. Doubts about the GLC have crossed the party divide. Throughout the 1970s London Conservatives were edged towards support for abolition of the GLC. Conservative boroughs saw abolition as a way of protecting their own local policies and preferences against a future inter-ventionist and socialist GLC. Under the leadership of Geoffrey Finsberg London Conservatives had produced plans for abolishing the GLC while the Conservative GLC had, more cautiously, engaged Sir Frank Marshall to inquire into London's local government and the role of the GLC (Young, 1984b, p. 5). In the 1977 borough

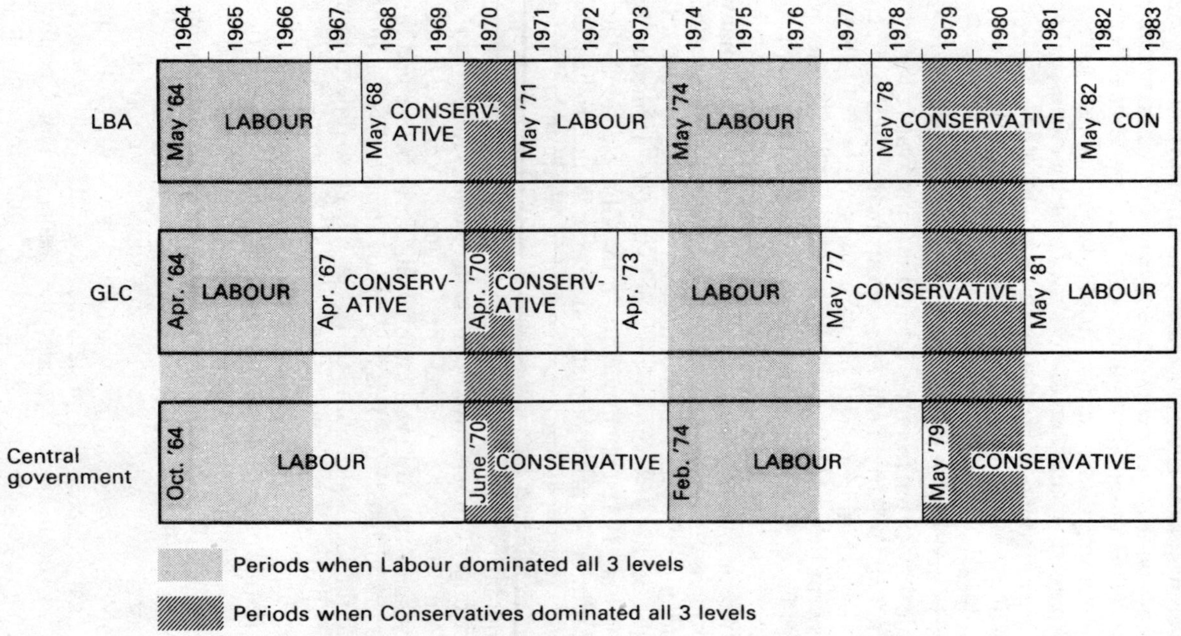

Figure 3.1 *The political profile of central and London Government 1964–84.*

LBA	GLC	Central government

LBA: May '64 LABOUR · May '68 CONSERVATIVE · May '71 LABOUR · May '74 LABOUR · May '78 CONSERVATIVE · May '82 CON

GLC: Apr. '64 LABOUR · Apr. '67 CONSERVATIVE · Apr. '70 CONSERVATIVE · Apr. '73 LABOUR · May '77 CONSERVATIVE · May '81 LABOUR

Central government: Oct. '64 LABOUR · June '70 CONSERVATIVE · Feb. '74 LABOUR · May '79 CONSERVATIVE

Periods when Labour dominated all 3 levels

Periods when Conservatives dominated all 3 levels

elections thirty-one candidates stood on an abolitionist platform, though none was elected. The issue remained live and ready to move on to the political agenda when the Conservatives lost control of the GLC in 1981.

Evaluating the performance of the GLC

Performance in local government is difficult both to assess and to compare. In the first place what are the appropriate objectives against which performance should be measured? Second, what constitutes an appropriate measure of performance? For the purposes of this discussion the starting-point will be the evaluative statements prefacing the proposals in *Streamlining the Cities* (DoE, 1983). However, the case presented there is in outline only and it is necessary to develop it having regard both to features of local government performance which the government has publicly favoured and to other features of performance which practitioners and commentators have singled out as indicative.

The White Paper suggests four areas of performance in which the GLC has fallen short of expectations. First, in discharging its functions it is said to have had too little regard for economy and efficiency (paras 1.3–1.5 and 1.13–1.17). Second, it has failed as a strategic body (para. 1.11). Third, it has generated conflict within the local government system (paras 1.11 and 1.12). Fourth, it is implied that the GLC is remote and inaccessible and out of touch with the real needs of the area it serves (paras 1.9 and 1.11).

Economy and Efficiency in London Government

Profligacy is the main charge against the GLC and the other metropolitan authorities. They are said to have imposed a 'heavy and unnecessary burden on ratepayers' (DoE, 1983, para. 5) by failing to give adequate weight to value for money, failing to cut manpower adequately, consistently overspending and trying to expand their role inappropriately. In order to assess the accuracy of this charge it is useful to ask three questions. First, how expensive are GLC services compared to those provided elsewhere? Secondly, to what extent do GLC services reflect duplication and empire-building rather than necessity and need? Third, how effectively has the GLC provided such services?

The comparison of per capita spending on services is made difficult by the fact that the costs of provision vary between areas and the costs also relate to the nature and quality of services delivered. Bearing such factors in mind do GLC services appear to be unduly costly? Per capita costs for most of the main services are shown in Appendix 3. In 1982/3 the GLC spent half as much per head on economic development and promotion as the other metropolitan counties, though considerably more than the shire counties. In 1983/4 the GLC planned to spend eight times as much in this area as the previous year. Since boroughs can also spend in this area overall spending on the service stands to exceed £9 per head in inner London – more than is spent on concessionary fares.

Education spending by ILEA per head exceeded that for all other types of authority by nearly a quarter in 1982/3 and the differential was due to increase to nearer a third in 1983/4. The comparison is often made between the cost of education in ILEA and the outer London boroughs. The former has fewer school-age children in the population but a high level of need. For example, three times as many ILEA pupils are entitled to free school meals. Need is used to justify lower pupil–teacher ratios, and higher costs per pupil/student than anywhere else in the country.

London's fire service costs more to provide, but it has a far greater proportion of its area categorized as 'high risk' requiring extra protection. The GLC spends far less on highway maintenance than other counties per capita, though in terms of investment per mile of road far more. This may relate to the greater demands for maintenance on London's busy roads. The picture for public transport is radically different; direct and indirect (through concessionary fares) subsidy in London is ten times that in the shire counties where public transport is dominated by the National Bus Company. The GLC provides the lion's share of the subsidy, as is the case in the metropolitan counties where subsidy is at a similar level; how well such money is spent is a matter of considerable controversy. The government argues that all subsidy is undesirable and levels should be minimized. Others argue that it is money well spent in terms of increasing usage of public transport and improving services thus reducing congestion and accidents as well as contributing to various social benefits. The scale of benefits demonstrated in the consultant's report on the MCCs is discussed in Chapter 4 (Coopers and Lybrand Associates, 1983).

The GLC spends relatively little per head on land use planning compared with other counties and less than the boroughs. A major increase was planned on such spending between 1982/3 and 1983/4 with the increased work planned on the revision of the Greater London Development Plan (GLDP).

As elsewhere, the GLC spends only a small proportion of the total spent on recreation, though it is rather more generous than some of the other counties. The GLC supports many national facilities such as the South Bank Arts complex as well as major sporting facilities such as Crystal Palace. The final service on the table, waste disposal, is also more expensive in per capita terms than elsewhere. The capital's rubbish is on a scale beyond that of any other city and the GLC has invested considerably in modern reduction facilities and has a variety of schemes including land infill on the lower Thames. Some of the facilities are partially privatized.

There is no concrete proof in these figures that the GLC is wasteful or spending unnecessarily. What they reveal are differences in costs of providing standard services, differences in need for services, and differences in the quantity and quality of services provided. The case against the GLC is that it is providing services of a sort which London neither needs nor deserves. This is a value judgement about the overall policies of the authority, disguised as a technical point about efficiency.

Another charge subsequently made against the GLC is that where it shares power with the boroughs for a particular service it tends to duplicate what the lower tier does. The main example of such duplication is highways where the boroughs act as agents of the GLC for construction and repairs to metropolitan roads. Proposals are discussed and evaluated in detail by both levels of government, a process which must inevitably contribute to their cost. In other fields the two tiers have developed complementarily, for example in the arts. The GLC has traditionally funded the national institutions located in London which were too expensive for individual boroughs to support; and latterly it has focused on minority groups which it has felt are ignored by boroughs.

The GLC may be an unwieldy and wasteful bureaucracy in certain respects, in others the boroughs may be small and inefficient service units. The argument in the White Paper is not only that the GLC is more prone to inefficiency than the boroughs, but also that it is engaged in empire-building to justify its existence. This is a charge that could be levelled against every authority that does more than its statutory minimum. It seems more likely to be an attack on the kinds of services which the GLC has developed and value judgements about their desirability. It is also a defence of central government and borough empire-building in fields such as housing, planning, transport and the police.

The GLC has been much criticized for its interest and involvement in aspects of public policy which central government considers to be none of its concern. It has upset both central government and the boroughs by demanding a key role in the accountability of the Metropolitan Police for which it has no responsibility. Although responsible for aspects of civil defence, it has angered government by its interest in defence issues and its anti-nuclear stance. Ken

Livingstone's personal approaches to 'unacceptable' Northern Ireland politicians also brought charges of meddling in matters of no concern to the GLC.

Where two authorities are involved in the same function planning and administration is replicated but this does not imply waste where neither authority could carry out the functions of the other as effectively. This is an argument for focusing on the service outputs from the GLC rather than its cash inputs. Could services of similar or better quality be obtained elsewhere than from the GLC? The GLC offers scale and breadth of vision which the boroughs cannot enjoy singly. It offers political will and commitment which consortia and appointed bodies cannot provide. Unfortunately, although it has probably done at least as well as any other system could have done in the circumstances, its record on service provision has been patchy. Planning has not got a grip on the problems of London's evolving city. Transport in London is hardly the envy of the world. The GLC has provided considerable housing stock but its quality and management have not been outstandingly good. In general the GLC has had the ability to muster technical and financial resources to provide good services but, as discussed below, for much of its life has been prisoner of its own self-doubts and rigidities within a hostile political environment.

However, the present arguments about efficiency and economy in the GLC are not really about value for money but about profound ideological differences relating to economic and public policy. The present GLC rejects both monetarism and privatization as appropriate policies for local government. It believes in expanding services and increasing public spending as a means of regenerating the economy, reducing unemployment and alleviating distress. It believes in municipalization and public or co-operative ownership. It rejects the appropriateness of the profit motive in the provision of public services, and it rejects notions of sole financial accountability to the ratepayer, placing the client equally high. This was the stance which was on trial in the action brought by Bromley BC with its famous (or infamous) interpretation of economic and fiduciary responsibility.

In the last years of its life the GLC has made a gesture towards central government by trimming its expenditure to fall nearer its target and thus claim some grant and reduce its precept marginally. London has always claimed that criticisms of its overspending are unfair because they do not take into account the subsidy provided to other parts of the country by the grant penalty system and ignore the redistribution of resources which the government has pursued between the urban and rural areas. Such factors have led the GLC and other critics of the abolition proposals to suggest that the only financially viable outcome of abolition will be a drastic reduction in local government services in London biting into those long accepted as needed and effective.

The GLC's Response to Key Issues in London

The White Paper suggested that strategic planning was a passing fashion and that in reality functions which need to be exercised at the wider level are few and far between. In order to evaluate this charge it is useful to look at the key issues in London over the life of the GLC which have called for some sort of strategic action and assess that authority's contribution to their solution.

London's economic base has changed dramatically during that period. There has been a decline in manufacturing and closure of key services such as the London docks. London has been a victim of national trends towards recession such as rising unemployment, though not to the degree that the older industrial areas of the North have been affected. For much of the time London has been subject to restrictions on commercial and industrial development in an attempt to shift development to worse areas of the country. The GLC has made efforts over the years to promote London but only recently, with the new Labour administration at County Hall and with a loosening by central government of locational policy, has the GLC attempted to tackle the problems of London's economic base directly. To do this it set up two initiatives: the Greater London Training Board involving employers, unions and the Manpower Services Commission, and the Greater London Enterprise Board which became a limited company in 1982 backed by GLC funding. Its role is to intervene to prevent closures and losses of jobs and to invest in socially useful industries operating on a democratic basis. Its overall impact on the economy has probably been marginal but it has had real impact on particular sectors and firms and on prospects in particular localities. Such mechanisms are of course in direct contrast to the government's preferred use of the market to achieve change.

Economic change connects with another area of strategic concern in London: rising levels of unemployment, poverty and dependence. Such patterns emerge from the demographic evolution of the city as much as from its economic decline. The GLC has approached these problems at both the symbolic and the practical level. Symbolically it has given welcome and support to campaigns such as the People's March for Jobs. Practically it has supported employment initiatives and attempted to improve the social wage provided by its services. For example, in the field of transport it has provided considerable subsidy for free travel for elderly people and special services for handicapped people. However, it has been suggested that the benefits of policies such as cheap underground fares have benefited commuters and workers more than the poorer and unwaged sectors of society (though the benefits in terms of environment and safety have been more widely distributed).

London's geography has been changing and parts of the capital have fallen into severe decline. At the beginning of the GLC's life it faced a tremendous property boom which wrought havoc on land and property prices. Speculation was rife, though eventually reduced by government intervention. Many of the older areas of London were in need of total refurbishment and in a period of very limited land supplies and high technology, solutions were sought in high-rise developments and new commercial centres. These areas, often vast impersonal municipal estates, have proved socially and environmentally unsatisfactory and in priority terms they have joined the remaining older and declining inner city areas.

The desire to intervene in the interests of inner city residents has raised two strategic issues for the GLC, first the question of intervention in areas of severe deprivation and second the question of redistribution of resources across an unequal metropolis. What might be the appropriate response of a strategic authority to the problems of particular areas? One role would be for the GLC itself to step in and identify and tackle the problems of certain neighbourhoods. This has been done in the past under the umbrella of Housing Action Areas and General Improvement Areas, and continues as a policy with the declaration of Community Areas. It has been criticized as an inappropriate role for a strategic authority and has shown no better results than projects undertaken by the boroughs (this begs the question of whether the boroughs would actually have undertaken the projects). A second role is for the GLC to work jointly with boroughs where there are problems of deprivation. Both tiers must of course work together in the context of the government's inner city partnership framework. However the voluntary joint arrangements involving the GLC and the boroughs in the Docklands area were largely unproductive because of internal wranglings and an Urban Development Corporation was imposed on the area in an attempt to get results. In the last few years there has been an increase in the level of joint activity with certain boroughs (usually Labour and usually containing deprived areas) on specific projects rather than in particular areas.

The problems of deprived neighbourhoods can be seen as part of the wider strategic issues of inequality. There has been considerable debate as to whether the appropriate response to such problems should be based on areas or groups. In London it almost certainly has to be both; there are wide differences in needs and resources between

areas of London and thus between London boroughs. One effect of
the existence of the GLC is for the opportunities for equalization to
grow with its role. Recognizing this, the ALA has demanded an
increased role for the GLC and powers for the GLC to act as
distributors of such resources as Housing Investment Programme
money. It is a factor which has always made Conservatives suspicious
of the GLC, and it is a factor which makes many boroughs nervous of
the impact of abolition. Although only a minority of GLC spending is
to be transferred to the boroughs and the government has promised
an extended rate equalization scheme and various safeguards, the
extra requirements are likely to have a severe impact on many
authorities (Travers, 1984).

Housing is the most appropriate service to evaluate in terms of
tackling underlying problems of geographical equality. Central to the
housing problem has been the lack of congruence in the maps of land
availability, housing demand and political will to build. The
problem involves an inner/outer imbalance and a north/south,
east/west imbalance. A classic study of the field (Young and Kramer,
1978, p. 213) concludes that:

> The Greater London Council failed to 'open up the suburbs'
> during the first ten years of its life. It incurred successive defeats on
> land use issues in both inner and outer London, and the housing
> cut-backs of 1975 signalled the end of the third major attempt in
> the space of a decade to achieve a more equitable distribution of
> urban space. The apparent recovery of a sense of strategic will
> between 1975 and 1977 rekindled hopes of new policy initiatives to
> that end. But the Conservative victory at the 1977 GLC election
> completed yet another cycle of change. Suburban exclusivity is
> once again guaranteed.

In the period that followed the GLC handed over most of its housing
stock to the boroughs and a new search began for a strategic housing
role in the GLC's more limited capacity. The impact on patterns of
inequality was negligible.

The policies of successive GLC administrations have had an
impact on different sectors of the population. Those benefiting from
Labour and Conservative GLCs have generally alternated between
the employed white working class and the middle classes. Business
has clearly taken its cut from London, quite handsomely at times.
However, Ken Livingstone's GLC has made it a priority to attempt to
reach groups and minorities who have not benefited in the past. This
could also be seen as a response to another strategic issue for London,
the implications of cultural and racial diversity.

GLC has been foremost among local authorities paying special attention to the needs of women, ethnic minorities and other groups suffering from disadvantage and discrimination. Committees and advisers have been brought in to examine the implications of council policies for such groups. This has resulted in changed working practices and reorientation of services, for example in the recipients of support for the arts and voluntary activities. Such policies are seen as very important by the Labour administration. They have been ridiculed in the press, particularly in London's evening newspaper the *Standard*, and have been an easy butt for Conservative boroughs.

A final strategic issue which the GLC has had to deal with has been the problems of London's basic infrastructure. London's present morphology dates back before the last war and key features of many areas to the last century or earlier. Its road and sewerage systems are under stress; public transport is costly and often overcrowded; public facilities such as wholesale markets have had to be relocated; and technological change makes ever-increasing impacts on an ageing conurbation. In so far as the state socializes such expenditure it is generally central government which takes the role of provider of such support to capitalist production. The big projects with which the GLC has been involved, such as the Thames Barrier, have been largely financed by central government. In fact the GLC has often been frustrated in its attempts to promote very large infrastructure projects such as a new underground line for the Docklands area or bids to capture international sporting events such as the Olympics. Many of the major highway problems such as the notorious south circular road are out of the hands of the GLC as a highway authority.

The GLC's success in responding to such issues has been attenuated by the 'flawed design' referred to earlier. Young and Kramer (1978) suggest that three problems have beset the GLC's attempts to develop an effective metropolitan strategy for London's housing, ambiguity of role, pendulum politics and problems in implementation. Scanning the history of the GLC more widely, two further factors might be added – limits of political acceptability and the role of central government.

The White Paper singles out the first of these factors as being central to the failure of the metropolitan counties (para. 1.11). Certainly the 'flawed design' identified in previous chapters has been a major problem for the GLC. The inheritance from the executive LCC, the location of detailed executive responsibilities at the county level, the need to undertake strategic planning under the pre-structure planning development plan process, all contributed to a tendency to retreat from strategic responses and strategic issues.

A persuasive argument for such a retreat is that central government has itself subsumed all key strategic roles in London. It retains the key resource allocation roles in housing and transport and it intervenes freely in major proposals such as major developments in central London, which might be thought of as the province of a strategic authority. The heart of this problem lies in the sheer scale and visibility of London government.

Pendulum politics, a characteristic of London's overall local government system illustrated earlier, means that there has been a lack of continuity in GLC policy. Strategic issues frequently require long-term policy application. Many of the key strategic issues are issues of high political salience and thus susceptible to radical changes of policy with changes in administration. Studies of British government suggest that administrators provide a basic continuity across regimes and that swings of policy are more rhetorical than real. Even if that is so (though there are areas where policy reversal is clearly real) it may imply another less desirable feature of government – unimaginative, unexceptionable policies which are acceptable to all shades of opinion and which do not run counter to the interests of the outer boroughs' residents. It can be argued that the political instability of London and the firmly entrenched interests of business, capital and the middle classes, preclude a whole range of strategic responses to strategic issues. In particular they preclude a radical redistributive role in relation to fundamental inequalities. Writers such as Dunleavy have argued that English metropolitan government was carefully designed in such a way as to make redistribution difficult. The boundaries were drawn tightly round the metropolitan area in a classic pattern of containment. The GLC's housing and planning powers were framed in such a way that they were always susceptible to the influence of the Conservative outer boroughs, even when a Labour government was in power (Dunleavy, 1980).

As a result of this and its own internal failings over the years, the GLC has always had difficulty implementing the strategic policies that it has developed. It has been inept at soliciting borough support for many policies and failed to appreciate the nature of borough politics. In the key areas of housing and planning it has failed to establish a first-class data base from which it could develop convincing policies, or even update the GLDP adequately.

What has seemed so alarming about Ken Livingstone's administration is that it has actually begun to break out of some of these binds and has argued strongly for the rest to be broken. The action brought by Bromley BC against the GLC for its Fares Fair policy was fuelled by alarm at the implications of the GLC pursuing a tough and radical policy such as had not been seen since Horace Cutler determined to transfer housing stocks to the boroughs whether they liked it or not. What has unnerved the government is that this could be done in defiance of its own policies and controls and with a majority of the boroughs Conservative. Enough vested interests feel threatened by the prospect of radically redistributive policies to give the abolition proposals an attractiveness far beyond their intrinsic merit.

Co-operation and Conflict in London's Government

Central government's analysis of conflict within the metropolitan system of local government is that it stems from the upper-tier authorities' search for a wider strategic role which the boroughs must implement. Such an analysis begs the question of the fundamental basis of such inter-authority conflicts and thus sheds little light on whether the present two-tier system exacerbates or mitigates such conflicts. It also assumes that the dysfunctions of the conflicts, which undoubtedly do occur, outweigh the positive contributions which inter-authority co-operation in the same system makes to the public good.

Research into the two-tier system of government in London and elsewhere demonstrates that inter-tier conflict is not endemic, but surrounds certain problematic tasks and concentrates in certain authorities. Furthermore, the system seems capable of containing constructively quite considerable amounts of policy difference without threatening the legitimacy and functioning of the system as a whole. Conflict between the GLC and the boroughs arises in a variety of situations. One such situation is where the supposedly strategic authority, the GLC, is involved in determining matters of local detail. Whether such matters can be construed as having strategic importance is irrelevant; the involvement of County Hall is seen as inappropriate and undesirable by the primary local authorities. Boroughs feel they are blamed by the public for the consequences of local actions regardless of which authority instigated them. The GLC is also, sometimes rightly, accused of having insufficient local understanding to take a satisfactory decision. Here, conflict is found where the GLC has powers to implement decisions relating to its core strategic functions rather than where it has strayed into new waters.

An example of such conflict can be seen in the field of transport where the GLC is the traffic management authority for all roads including those maintained by the boroughs. The boroughs must petition and persuade the GLC of the need for a pedestrian crossing or parking restrictions in a local centre. The GLC would claim that its role was justified because of the knock-on effects of any intervention in the traffic flow, and the need for a standard and safe highway system. The boroughs would argue that they are the authorities which understand local traffic problems and to which angry motorists, pedestrians and residents look for a solution. They would claim that they have sufficient expertise to undertake traffic management functions and carry them out in a widely satisfactory way.

Planning is another area where the boroughs are to a greater or lesser extent resentful of the GLC's involvement in detail through the development control process. Efforts on the part of the LBA and others to get the secretary of state to bring London development control powers in line with the rest of the country have so far failed. A typical outer London borough may find itself referring a hundred planning applications (about 5 per cent of the total handled) to the GLC. If a borough wants to give permission for a development which falls under the prescribed headings it must be referred to the GLC who then go through a similar process of consideration culminating in a joint members meeting which advises the GLC's committee if the two authorities adopt a different stance. Not only do boroughs resent the GLC overriding their recommendations but also they complain at the use of the system to modify and develop the strategic planning base, the GLDP, as some would say, by stealth. It is also seen as lengthening and duplicating the planning process.

Development control is a forum where a variety of conflicts in the system overlay one another. It also has a particular significance in the system. It is the main forum where members from the two levels interact and because, by definition it is founded upon dispute, members receive a very unrepresentative impression of the extent of conflict between the tiers. It is also an area which touches upon the key bases of class and interest, in other words, land and property (Saunders, 1979). The kind of application likely to be referred to the GLC may (though not necessarily) involve millions of pounds in commercial or other development as well as involving considerable rate income.

Conflict also arises between the tiers because the GLC and the boroughs must inevitably pursue different objectives and have different priorities. Local authorities have considerable autonomy in terms of how they carry out their duties and the priorities they set for their services. Professionals and politicians in the GLC may see things one way, those in the boroughs may see them another. In part this reflects politics and ideologies; it also reflects the difference in scale and purpose of the two tiers. This is illustrated by conflicts which have surrounded strategic planning in London. The original proposals for the GLDP with its particular blend of highway and development proposals for London as a whole was no more acceptable to many boroughs than recent proposals for a revised development plan with its emphasis on renewal of London's inner ring and restriction of development in other zones. Such conflicts are the natural result of articulating the interests of very different groups and areas.

A further cause of conflict is the gross difference in size between the GLC and the boroughs, and their different ways of operating. Boroughs complain of the bureaucracy of the GLC, its slowness, the number of staff to be dealt with, its remoteness and its insularity. The GLC complains of the parochial attitude of boroughs, their inability or unwillingness to understand how the GLC works and their failure to make use of the services it offers. There are examples, often of quite minor tasks, where the two tiers have spent endless time and energy disputing how something should be done. For example, ever since its inception the GLC has been arguing with the boroughs about the collection of planning information. Roomfuls of paperwork have accumulated at the GLC which have produced little useful information. The GLC blames the boroughs for providing incomplete and late data and not filling forms in correctly. The boroughs blame the GLC for its cumbersome system and lack of useful output. Twenty years and endless meetings later the system has been improved somewhat while in the mean time most of the boroughs have set up their own independent information systems, making parts of the system redundant.

The GLC has indeed adopted a cavalier attitude to the boroughs at times. Its extraordinary lack of sensitivity to borough problems and politics was shown particularly clearly when it levied its supplementary rate in 1981 with little or no consultation with the boroughs. In particular it embarrassed Labour boroughs who had to dispatch the demands for a further rate while endeavouring against central government pressure to maintain their own spending.

Another cause of conflict lies not in any particular action of the GLC but in a more generalized antipathy on the part of certain boroughs to another authority impinging on their work, and on the part of some boroughs to the Labour Party and a Labour GLC. All boroughs, to a greater or lesser degree, see themselves as potentially all-purpose authorities, able to carry out most of the tasks of local government. Their predecessors fought against the creation of the GLC and two decades later, despite the present public defence of the GLC by many Labour boroughs, they still resent its ability to override their decisions and curb some of their ambitions. Many Conservative boroughs have had long and fruitful relationships with the GLC traversing several regimes, which continue underneath the public rhetoric of opposition. Many probably resent central government's interference with their autonomy as much as the GLC's but the rules of politics do not permit such feelings to be proclaimed publicly in the same way. It is all the more remarkable, therefore, to find Conservative boroughs declaring themselves against the proposals for abolition.

Town Hall versus County Hall becomes news whereas the times

they are working together goes unreported. Co-operation goes beyond simply 'doing their best to make the system work' (DoE, 1983, para. 1.17). The GLC and the boroughs have made common cause against proposals which would have affected both adversely. They have also set up joint projects which neither could achieve by themselves. This has been the case particularly with the present Labour administration in County Hall. They have made considerable funds available for local community and employment projects in conjunction with interested boroughs. The GLC obviously exploited its position of being above government penalties (it had no rate support grant to remove because of its high spending) to assist boroughs – mostly Labour but a few Conservative – who had projects and programmes they could not fund themselves.

Co-operation is not simply about special projects. In many service areas the two tiers have used their resources and skills in a complementary way to achieve a particularly high level of service. For example the boroughs and the Historical Buildings Division of the GLC have together created a unique specialist service in relation to the capital's architectural heritage. Most boroughs benefit from the purchasing service operated by the GLC which offers them substantial discounts on supplies.

There is an assumption in the White Paper that if the GLC is abolished conflict will decrease and co-operation will increase in the London government system. Such an assumption not only justifies the proposal to abolish but also justifies the voluntary arrangements which would replace the GLC. Research into the two-tier system only partially confirms this. Abolition will remove the conflicts based on jealousy, misunderstanding and awkward divisions of power between the tiers. However, it will not remove conflicts rooted in ideological difference and the conflicts between local needs and preferences and the needs and preferences of London as a whole. It will also shift the basis for co-operation from two types of authorities with complementary skills and resources to similar types of authorities, and from co-operation between small numbers of authorities to co-operation between large numbers. Both shifts are likely to make co-operation more difficult and less rewarding.

Accountability of London's Government

It is implied in the White Paper that the system of accountable control in the metropolitan areas has failed. It is suggested that authorities such as the GLC are remote, inaccessible, prone to pursuing irrelevant policies and little understood by the public. Furthermore, direct accountability for various London-wide decisions is not valued highly and is disregarded in the arrangements proposed after abolition.

In fact there is little evidence to support any of these allegations in London. Indicators of healthy local democracy would include higher than expected electoral turnout, elections fought on local issues, after strong public debate. Turnout at the 1981 GLC election was good by local government standards, as Table 3.1 shows: 44·1 per cent compared with 66·5 per cent at the 1979 general election in the same constituencies. Labour captured the GLC on the basis of 41·8 per cent of votes cast, a reasonable figure by parliamentary standards. The present government secured only 44 per cent of votes and was positively endorsed by fewer than 30 per cent of London's eligible voters.

Table 3.1   *Turnout at GLC election 1981*

Poll turnout (%)	No. of constituencies	%
30–34	7	7·6
35–39	16	17·4
40–44	32	34·8
45–49	24	26·1
50–54	11	11·9
55–59	1	1·1
60–64	1	1·1

There was much debate when Bromley made its challenge to the GLC's supplementary rate in the High Court as to whether the GLC had been given a mandate by Londoners to carry out policies contrary to those being pursued by central government. It is debatable whether any government or administration in recent times has had a definite mandate to carry out particular policies. Mrs Thatcher's own governments have been positively endorsed by a minority of the electorate and endorsement has been on the basis of a broad slate of possible programmes and policy directions. The Labour manifesto for the 1981 election set out quite clearly the set of policies and programmes which offended the government – increased GLC spending, fare reductions, new council housing building, a Greater London Enterprise Board, a police committee and rejection of civil defence work. Londoners were not misled about the direction of future Labour policy, though they were to be misled as to who would lead a Labour London – Ken Livingstone unseated the moderate Andrew Mackintosh the day after the election.

The election took place against the backdrop of the Brixton riots and a low point in Mrs Thatcher's popularity. The issues received widespread local and national media coverage. The campaign may not have been exciting but it was visible (Cousins, 1982). In many ways it was a national phenomenon reflecting judgement on central government's performance, but in its key issues – transport and housing – and in certain results – the failure of 'Red Ted' to be elected – it was a London event. These characteristics matter because they give the GLC the ability to claim to represent the views and preferences of Londoners on local government issues as well as, if not better than, central government.

The government case is that the two-tier system of government in metropolitan areas is difficult to understand (DoE, 1983, para. 1.19). It also implies some form of false consciousness on the part of those who voted in the Labour administration in its rejection of the validity of many GLC policies. The GLC as part of its anti-government stance has spent a great deal of money on publicity. Some of it has been of a simple information-giving nature and a raising of the profile of the GLC, some of it has been heavily ideological and outright propaganda against government restrictions and against abolition. Combined with the high political profile of Ken Livingstone it has created considerable awareness of the GLC. This has probably contributed to the support for the GLC revealed by opinion polls.

A MORI poll commissioned by the London *Standard* in March 1984 revealed, as previous polls, a good degree of satisfaction with the GLC and doubts about government intentions to abolish it: 61 per cent of Londoners disapproved of abolition compared with 22 per cent who approved; 53 per cent were satisfied with the way the GLC was running London, though satisfaction with Ken Livingstone's leadership was lower at 43 per cent. While 55 per cent of people thought that abolition would put their rates up, only 15 per cent thought services would improve and only 20 per cent thought better government for London would result.

Accountability has been a major issue in the debate about the Labour GLC's policies. Critics argue that it has paid insufficient attention to those financing the system – domestic and non-domestic ratepayers – and too much attention to clients and the beneficiaries of services. This is not as implied in the White Paper a failure to check waste and promote efficiency but a deliberate socialist policy aimed at redistributing forms of income. The GLC has attempted to lay to rest for ever the legacy of the ratepayer franchise upon which modern local government was built (Loughlin, 1983). The judgement of the House of Lords in favour of Bromley BC in the fares case, with its emphasis on fiduciary responsibility, also checked such tendencies but in no way reversed them.

Abolition will, as presently proposed, make local government more confusing by proliferating *ad hoc* bodies and do little to strengthen accountability because of the introduction of non-elected and indirectly elected bodies. By comparison the GLC has a justification for claiming public support and a defensible link between its policies and the electorate. Accountability has not failed in London: the electorate have exercised their right to choose but unfortunately their choice is one which central government ideology no longer permits.

The future of London's Local Government

London has led the way in the development of British metropolitan government and has been central to proposals for its abolition. Paradoxically London is the area most capable of demonstrating the necessity to rethink the strategy of abolition.

The thrust of the 1983 White Paper would be to create a system of local government unique among the major Western cities of the size and prominence of London. No other capital is without its metropolitan-wide authority concerned with the development and servicing of the city as a whole (Norton, 1983). Many observers and commentators suggest that London also needs such arrangements.

Apart from the retention at metropolitan level of various former GLC functions through joint boards, *ad hoc* bodies and special schemes, various other proposals have been made to overcome the dysfunctions of abolition. A directly elected assembly for London has been a popular proposal with a number of groups including the Conservative group on the GLC. Proponents of the idea have been careful to distinguish the new assembly from the existing GLC, though it is generally suggested that such an assembly would cover broadly the same functions as the GLC and would in many ways resemble a local authority.

The popularity of such a proposal stems from the problems of devolving power satisfactorily to thirty-three lower-tier authorities in London and the consequent absorption of many former GLC functions by central government. Transport is a major example of such centralization, other services such as strategic planning and land drainage are being closely tied into central control mechanisms by the proposals. This has led to the proposal that government of London be given special recognition in the parliamentary system by the establishment of a parliamentary committee such as a Grant Committee of London MPs (Swaffield, 1984). Patrick Jenkin's September proposal for an Assembly consisting of London MPs falls far short of creating a local authority. It is unlikely that such a proposal is popular with parliamentarians but it highlights the problem of accountability in London where scale and need have made centralization the only feasible strategy for abolition.

4 Metropolitan County Councils: The First Ten Years

In the Government's view, a metropolitan type of structure would be appropriate in Merseyside, SELNEC, West Midlands and in addition, in West Yorkshire, South Yorkshire and the Tyne and Wear area. These six areas need to be treated as entities for the purpose of planning, transportation and certain other services.

(Cmnd 4584/71, *Local Government in England*, HMSO, 1971)

Introduction

Without the existence and recent activities of the GLC, it is highly unlikely that the existence of the MCCs themselves would have been threatened. They have, perhaps, rather unluckily been included in the abolition proposal because of their structural and functional similarity to the GLC and, as several have argued, because they all at the moment happen to be Labour-controlled (Talk by Pauley, 1984). However, although by and large the Labour politicians who currently held power in the MCCs are different in ideology and style from those who held power between 1973 and 1977, their activities have proved less controversial than those of the GLC. Some policies similar to those in the GLC have been developed and similar causes espoused in the MCCs particularly, perhaps, in Merseyside and West Midlands. South Yorkshire was in dispute with the Department of Transport over its level of fares subsidies in 1977 (that is well before the GLC was) and has continued to be so ever since. But generally and particularly in the area of 'interventionist' policy initiatives, MCCs have adopted a lower-key approach and disputes with the Conservative government have been less intense than those of the GLC. All are deemed on the government's criteria to be over-spending, but not at the same level as the GLC. Merseyside and South Yorkshire are included in the list of eighteen authorities to be rate-capped, but not the other MCCs. The inclusion of the MCCs almost as 'makeweights' to the GLC is ironic because the case for retention of a metropolitan-wide level of government is clearly stronger in the GLC than elsewhere (see Chapter 3).

The Political Profile of the MCCs

The MCCs, like the GLC, have alternated between periods of Conservative and Labour control (with the exception of Tyne and Wear and South Yorkshire, which have always been Labour controlled). However, again like the GLC, it has been uncommon for there to be political congruence among the three levels of government in metropolitan areas – national, metropolitan and district (on a majority basis). As Figure 4.1 shows, the years of national/ metropolitan political congruence have been few with the same party being in power at both levels only in the periods 1974–6 and 1979–81 (South Yorkshire and Tyne and Wear excepted). During the first of these periods Labour was also in control in a large majority of metropolitan district councils (MDCs) in each of the metropolitan areas. During the second, the pattern was more complex, with three of the six having a majority of MDCs with Conservative control in 1979–80, but the balance shifting to five out of six having a majority of MDCs with Labour control by 1980–1. Hence only in three out of their ten years of existence have MCCs enjoyed support from the same political party at national and district level simultaneously. This has undoubtedly hampered their ability to perform effectively many of the functions allocated to them.

As in London and elsewhere, the politics of the second-tier authorities has become much more sharply polarized since 1981. Moderate Labour and Conservative MDCs still exist but there is a clear trend towards control by the new left (for example, in Manchester, Liverpool, Sheffield and, up to 1982, Walsall) or the new right (for example, in Trafford, Wirral, Birmingham and Dudley). These differences have affected the stance of the MDCs to *Streamlining the Cities*. It is Labour Party policy to oppose the abolition proposals and to refuse to co-operate in the transitional arrangements. This has been followed in all Labour-controlled MDCs (with a certain amount of internal heart-searching, especially in the big cities). The relatively few Conservative-controlled MDCs support the abolition proposals with (as in London) varying degrees of enthusiasm.

One of the major differences between the GLC and the MCCs lies in the number of second-tier authorities involved. In Chapter 3, the important role of the London Boroughs Association in a situation where there are thirty-three lower-tier authorities is discussed. Although collective intermediaries do exist in some of the MCCs (occasionally including – as in Greater Manchester – the county council itself) their role is much less significant, reflecting the much smaller number of lower-tier authorities concerned (varying from ten in Greater Manchester to four in South Yorkshire) and their larger areas of populations (compared with the London boroughs).

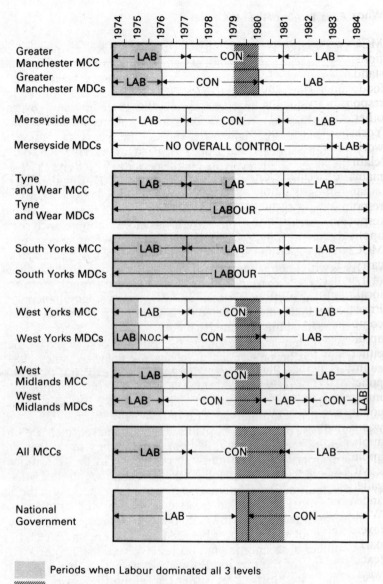

Figure 4.1 *Political control in the United Kingdom, the MCCs and the MDCs 1974–84.*

Who Does What in the Metropolitan Areas?

MCCs are wholly responsible for police (with important qualifications, see Chapter 2), the fire service, refuse disposal, trading standards, consumer protection (for example, weights and measures, food and drink) and public transport. They have the statutory responsibility for the construction and maintenance of roads, and other highway and traffic functions but have all (except West Yorkshire) permitted the MDCs to carry out a significant part of this work under agency agreements (in some cases district councils have 'claimed' under Section 187 of the Local Government Act 1972 to maintain urban unclassified roads).

Land-use planning is a shared function, the MCC being responsible for structure planning and (since 1981) having sole responsibility for minerals and refuse disposal sites. All other applications are dealt with by the MDCs which must consult the MCCs over applications of strategic significance. Both tiers may carry out local planning, although in practice the MDCs do the bulk of it, with the MCCs having the power to withhold 'certification' of a local plan if it is not in accordance with the county structure plan. Prior to 1980 the land-use planning was divided in a much more complex way. The MCCs then had responsibility for planning applications involving strategic matters, that is applications which either were of major significance in relation to the provisions of the county structure plan (or prior to that, agreed interim planning policies) or represented significant departures from it. The scope for interpretation in the provision meant that it was not always easy for county and district to agree what was a strategic matter, and indeed it was sometimes difficult for a county to get hold of a contentious application and to make a judgement on it, given that all planning applications were first received by the district.

MCCs have concurrent powers with districts for museums and art galleries, which they exercise almost exclusively in some cases (Tyne and Wear, Merseyside) and hardly at all in others (West Yorkshire, West Midlands). There are similar provisions for recreation (exercised in limited fashion everywhere apart from some county parks, and sponsorship of events); and economic development (exercised enthusiastically by all the MCCs and MDCs – in various ways). MDCs have exclusive responsibility for education, social services, libraries, housing, refuse collection and environmental health. This means, as the authors of *Streamlining the Cities* were eager to point out, that MDCs determine the bulk of expenditure – around 74 per cent – in metropolitan areas, and of course, are the rating authorities with MCCs issuing precepts.

The main areas of contact between MCCs and MDCs are therefore over land-use planning, highways construction and maintenance and traffic management, waste processing usually (though not necessarily) over the concurrent functions of arts, recreation and economic development, and over the issue of the precept. There are also a number of minor areas which may be of mutual concern, for example civil defence, joint purchasing, gypsy sites and archives. The experience of these areas of shared or contingent responsibility will be explored later in this chapter.

The Metropolitan Counties as Strategic Authorities

How have the MCCs attempted to exercise their emasculated strategic role, and how well have they succeeded? As we have seen, the Redcliffe-Maud conception of the strategic role focused on the interrelated activities of land-use planning and transportation (highways and public transport). Had the economic development function been seen as significant at the time, it is probable that this also would have been allocated to the MCCs (see Redcliffe-Maud, 1969, para. 331). The recent Stodart Committee, evaluating the allocation of functions between regions and districts in Scotland certainly developed the view that such powers should be exclusively in the hands of the regions (Stodart Committee, 1981, pp. 43–4). In the event, MCCs have had to share planning and economic development powers with MDCs, they have had virtually no housing powers, and highway construction and maintenance, though clearly their statutory responsibility, has been operated on an agency basis in most metropolitan counties. In several respects, the performance by the MCCs of their strategic role has shown a significant improvement on the efforts of previous institutional arrangements involved (see examples discussed in D. T. Cross and Bristow, 1983). Because public transport, highways and land-use planning have been (with certain important provisos) within the jurisdiction of the same authority (the MCC), it has proved possible both to make choices between priorities (for example, public transport versus new road-building) and to co-ordinate the development of facilities in a way which was much more difficult prior to 1974. More problematical have been the lack of effective control mechanisms in the field of land-use planning and, to a lesser extent, highways.

Looking specifically at the exercise of the strategic role in land-use planning, the MCCs have had a difficult task. The experience of the shared planning responsibility in Greater London (G. Rhodes, 1972, p. 337; Marshall, 1978, p. 15) did not argue well for the future of the same function in the rest of the country, especially when the problem of 'who did what' was left more open than in the London case, on both development control and local plans. The circular on planning in the new system (74/73, 'Co-operation between authorities') relied heavily on bland exhortations to exercise mutual goodwill and co-operation. There were a number of tactical options open however to the new MCC planning departments which had, incidentally, in most areas attracted some of the most able planners in pre-1974 counties and county boroughs involved. The responsibility to produce a county structure plan was clearly and unqualifiedly theirs. This involved however a period of some three or four years before it could hope to be approved, except in the West Midlands where the new county inherited a set of structure plans, produced in a rush prior to reorganization by the old county boroughs, which, to say the least, gave the impression of being stitched together at the (inter-county borough) edges (see Cross and Bristow, 1983, pp. 65–6). Once approved, a county structure plan stood to be a major advantage to the metropolitan counties in their responsibility to define and decide 'county matters'.

In the mean time (1974–8) the tactical options ranged from a 'hard-line' approach – the production of a number of interim policy statements and the attempt to define as 'county matters' any issue of significance relating to them – to a permissive one – the playing down of the idea of 'county responsibility' and the reliance upon the existence of the professional network to ensure 'good' planning decisions through behind-the-scenes liaison. In all the new metro-politan areas (most in Greater Manchester and Merseyside, least in Tyne and Wear and West Midlands) there was an extensive inter-tier network of personal and professional linkages in the land-use planning world, which could be used in this way. It was this course which provided the easier option, and was widely used (least so in West Yorkshire see Dixon, 1978, pp. 116 ff.). What tended to happen was that so long as the MDC planning department was prepared to recommend to its committee on an application which the MCC felt a 'county matter', a decision that was in line with county policy, then it was common for the county not to insist on deciding the application itself. Applications for large-scale office and shopping developments were the kind of issues typically involved. Alternatively, if there was an awareness in the MDC planning department that its planning committee might make an unwise decision over such an application (or indeed over an application which was less clearly a county matter), then it was not uncommon in certain MDCs for it to be designated a 'county matter' and passed on to the county.

With the benefit of hindsight these tactics were perhaps short-sighted in that they in effect played down the significance of the MCC as an explicit strategic decision-maker. There was, in fact, a power of direction which could be used by an MCC – a requirement imposed upon a district by a county to turn down a planning application in the interests of county policy – but this was rarely used in the metropolitan counties, with persuasion and behind-the-scenes discussion being much more popular tactics. The wheels were further oiled in most metropolitan county planning departments by the provision of specialist services, available free or at a limited charge to districts which required them. One of the problems, however, with permissive MCC tactics was that they assumed a level of co-operativeness on the part of the MDCs which did not always exist, either at political or officer level. Not only were applications involving county matters (for example, a sizeable new housing development) not always defined as such, or passed on readily to the MCC; but also advice to a district planning committee, agreed on the inter-tier professional grapevine, was sometimes overturned by the committee. There were two forces at work here. First, some though by no means all MDC planning officers wanted to limit their dependence on the MCC. A muted kind of interdepartmental rivalry was sometimes in operation. Secondly, in some MDCs there were political differences with the MCC over particular planning policies (for example, the City of Birmingham wanted more new office development in their city centre than West Midlands County Council thought desirable). In this case the politicians involved would try to reserve the decisions involved to the district, or failing that to use inter-tier political networks to try to persuade the county to make an exception.

One of the problems for the MCCs before 1981 was that there was not usually a particularly strong political commitment to the policies of the structure plan. Thus disputes developing at officer level and then entering the political arenas might well be lost. The nature of the disputes involved rarely reflected major differences of class interest within metropolitan areas. Attempts by the MCC to intrude upon the suburban amenity of some of the richer outer boroughs through overspill policies were conspicuous by their absence. To some extent, the decline in economic growth, and the then less polarized political stances reduced both the pressures for such policies and the commit-ment to them. Indeed the county structure plans which began to emerge in draft from around 1976 were not particularly contentious documents and within the metropolitan areas general agreement about the main lines of policy (for example, on emphasis on the regeneration of inner city areas) was often achieved, especially in West Midlands and on Merseyside. Differences were more likely to occur over locational priorities for investment expressed in structure plans, which clearly benefited one district rather than another (for example, the Dearne Valley emphasis in the South Yorkshire Structure Plan: see Darke, 1980).

In fact the major differences which emerged in some Structure Plan Examinations in Public were those between county and district councils (acting in concert) and some of the adjacent shire counties. The bitter fights between the West Midlands authorities (especially the county council and the district councils of Birmingham, Wolverhampton and Walsall) and Staffordshire over the Green Belt policy in the Staffordshire County Structure Plan were a vivid illustration of this (see Bridges and Vielba, 1976). In other words, because of the tightness of the MCC boundaries in 1974 potential class-based differences between MCC and MDC were transformed into class-based differences between shire county council and metropolitan county council.

There have also been similar problems with the equally 'grey' area of local plans. Indeed, since 1980, the withholding of certification of local plans drawn up by districts has been the major power left available to the metropolitan counties whereby they might implement their strategic land-use planning role. Prior to 1980, few local plans had been produced by metropolitan districts, reflecting the absence in most metropolitan areas until around 1977 or 1978 of an approved county structure plan. Such disputes that did arise in this area tended to be in connection with responsibility for local plans. The ownership of the Greater Manchester River Valley local plans provides an example, providing the basis for a series of county/district disputes about whose statutory responsibility such plans should be. Since 1980 there have been more examples of metropolitan counties attempting to exercise their strategic role by refusing to certify 'non-conforming' local plans; successfully in the cases of the Morley Local Plan (Leeds/West Yorkshire) and the Horwich Local Plan (Bolton/Greater Manchester) and more inconclusively in the case of Newcastle city centre (Newcastle/Tyne and Wear) and Cranmore-Widney (Solihull/West Midlands). It is significant that the DoE attitude to such disputes over the past two years has been to try to persuade counties not to withhold certification, but rather to appear with their objections at the local planning inquiry.

The other aspect of planning strategy which generated a good deal of unresolved tension was the question of whether the fact that a county structure plan had to deal with topics such as housing (a district responsibility) and recreation (a shared, but in the event heavily district-oriented function) allowed the county legitimate access to details of district activities in these fields and the right to produce an 'overarching' policy (for example, more clearance needed than proposed in District 'A'; more improvement in District 'B'), on the basis of their statutory responsibility for structure planning. Some districts took great exception to this 'interference' (as it was regarded). It was a major issue in West Yorkshire (see Dixon, 1978, pp. 121–5), and later in Greater Manchester where the former Chief Executive of Manchester has been quoted as saying that 'it made him feel ill to see the way in which the Structure Plan had been abused as an entrance into activities which were legitimately the District's responsibility' (S. N. Leach, 1984, p. 67).

In the event, although metropolitan counties might (and did) include policy statements about housing and recreation in their structure plans, there was little they could do to implement such policies. The main instrument for imposing this limitation was the DoE planning inspectorate who took a very narrow view about the appropriate content of structure plans. Private house-building could be 'encouraged' in locations earmarked as suitable but the public housing policies of the districts were impervious to county council influence, with the vague 'reserve housing powers' available to counties proving unexploited and probably unexploitable. Although certain aspects of recreational policy – for example, derelict land reclamation and the associated development of country parks (see especially the Greater Manchester River Valley projects: Maund, 1982) could be implemented by MCCs, the bulk of action and expenditure in recreation remained with the districts. Even in the field of economic development, although all the MCCs vigorously pursued their own policies, the MDCs did also, in ways which were not always compatible with county priorities (see Mawson, 1983).

Thus was the scope for county structure plans to act as effective strategic documents limited by their long gestation period, the lack (and subsequent further reduction in 1980) of development control powers, the lack of significant housing powers in the county and the shared nature of powers in recreation and economic development. To this can be added the relative shortage since 1974 of strategic land-use issues for county authorities to address. As was argued in Chapter 2, the metropolitan counties were designed in and for an era of economic growth and although 'strategic issues' can still be identified in a time of economic stagnation, they are different in nature from those associated with an era of economic growth. It can be argued that issues of decline and stagnation are not necessarily most appropriately tackled by the tool of a structure plan (as currently defined) which was designed to control and handle expansion. The need for the strategic role remains, but the most appropriate tools may well be different.

As John Stewart has pointed out, it is a mistake to equate the strategic planning role of an authority with its strategic land-use planning role (see Stewart, 1980). However, a strong strategic land-use planning role would have helped the MCCs establish their credibility as strategic authorities. Their inability to develop such a role, coupled with their lack of effective powers in other related fields (housing, resource allocation) has meant that they have been unable to measure up to Redcliffe-Maud's conception of strategic planning authorities either. Hence, if the metropolitan counties have failed to establish an effective strategic role it is to a large extent because they have not been given the tools.

Although the MCCs' achievements have been limited in relation to strategic planning in an overall sense, they have been more tangible in relation to transportation planning. Considerable progress has been made towards integrated public transport systems by the Passenger Transport Executives in all the MCCs. Innovations such as the Merseyside Loop and Link Rail system, the Tyne and Wear Metro and the West Midlands Cross-City link line, although conceived before the 1974 reorganization, have been successfully implemented and operated by the new MCCs. Devices such as national route planning, travel cards and through-ticketing schemes (for bus and rail) have all proved much more feasible to introduce under a single head of responsibility. As a recent piece of research shows (Gwilliam *et al.*, 1984) it is these kinds of achievements and further progress in connection with them which would be most threatened by the abolition of the MCCs and in particular by the possibility of districts running their own public transport services.

The possibility in metropolitan areas for strategic choices to be made over what kind of transport system is most appropriate has also been a major gain. The Transport Policies and Programmes (TPPs) submissions and structure plans of the MCCs since 1974 have demonstrated a reasoned justification for the policy proposals set out which was not apparent (or possible) before. First, the highways building programmes of the pre-1974 authorities in the metropolitan areas have been drastically curtailed, as inter-district competition over road-building has been eliminated and it has become possible to relate highways planning more realistically to overall population change. Secondly, all the MCCs in varying degrees have emphasized the provision of public transport as a solution to the problem of movement within metropolitan areas, and have moved away from the provision of major new road-building schemes as a policy priority.

The ability of the MCCs to develop and implement transportation strategies has of course been limited in various ways, especially by the increasing use of the TPP system as an attempt to impose central government priorities (see Skelcher *et al.*, 1983) and also by government curbs on capital expenditure. There have also been doubts expressed about the extent to which MCCs have succeeded in satisfactorily interrelating land-use planning and transport planning systems (that is, structure plans and TPPs). Their difficulties in this respect may have reflected not only the increasing constraints placed by central government of both processes, but also the fact that in most MCCs different pieces of departmental machinery are responsible for the two planning systems. None the less, the importance in principle of linking transport and planning in the metropolitan areas remains. It will undoubtedly become considerably more difficult, given the new institutional arrangements proposed by the government.

The Problem of Highways Agency Agreements

The criticism is made in *Streamlining the Cities* that the MCCs have had too little regard for economy and efficiency. One area of activity linked to the strategic function of land-use/transportation planning, where this accusation has some substance, is that of highways construction and maintenance. Elsewhere the government have argued that the GLC and the MCCs have 'full responsibility for only a limited number of functions'. Highways is presumably not one of the functions for which MCCs are deemed to have full responsibility because of the widespread use of agency arrangements, whereby MDCs carry out highways construction, maintenance and a range of other associated functions on an agency basis. This practice together with the arrangements over land-use planning has proved the most popular target for accusations of 'duplication and overlap'. The history of highways agencies which incidentally also provide the major example of the MCCs playing a resource-allocation role (see Chapter 2) is worth considering in more detail.

As soon as the agency provision in the 1972 Act became apparent and the circumstances under which agency arrangements were recommended were set out in the circular which followed (DoE, 1972, Circular 131/72), there was always a strong likelihood of most MDCs exercising highways agency powers. This resulted in the period just before reorganization, in many highways construction and maintenance engineers and manual workers choosing to remain with their current authorities rather than making the move to the unknown territory of a metropolitan county. As a result many MCCs found it hard to staff up with suitably qualified engineering personnel and would have found it very difficult in 1974 to carry out their duties in this field. The pressure to agree relatively generous (in terms of the amount of work to be done by districts) highways agencies was strong, and this is what happened in five of the six new metropolitan counties. Indeed one MCC chief executive claimed: 'Our highways agency was the most give-way agency you could possibly have' (quoted in Alexander, 1982, p. 61).

The exception was West Yorkshire where the previous existence of the West Riding of Yorkshire over roughly the territory of new metropolitan counties of West Yorkshire and South Yorkshire and the appointment of the Leeds City Engineer (and subsequently many of his staff) to a key position in the new West Yorkshire County Council hierarchy meant that staffing with appropriately skilled staff was much easier. As a result of a deal done at officer level (Dixon, 1978, p. 57) the districts in West Yorkshire made no claim for agency nor did they insist on their Section 187 (claiming) rights (Local Government Act 1972). The exception was Bradford which did claim, under this section, the right to maintain urban unclassified roads. As a result, in the whole of West Yorkshire apart from Bradford, the highways function was run as a unitary service by the county council from 1974 onwards. South Yorkshire County Council also inherited staff from the old West Riding, but here agency was granted to the district councils following considerable political pressure from them.

The problems facing the county councils which did concede highways agency are well illustrated by Hughes (1979) in his study of the history of highways agency in the West Midlands from 1974 to 1979. First, the allocation of resources between districts was a much more competitive process than it would have been without agency, with each metropolitan district arguing strongly for a generous allocation and certainly not less than was spent in their district the previous year. As a result, it proved much more difficult to allocate funds for (for example) highways maintenance on an objective basis. All MCCs had to modify the financial allocations implied by the MARCH or CHART process (an objective measure of the physical conditions of roads) because to do otherwise would have resulted in politically contentious switches of resources between one district and another. Secondly, it proved hard for the MCCs to control adequately the quality of work done. MDCs understandably wanted to be left to make their own decisions about the order of priority of accepted schemes, the nature of the materials used, and so on, and the counties, particularly in the early days, were reluctant to interefere too much. As a result, there were considerable disparities in the degree of efficiency of use of resources amongst metropolitan districts (see Hughes, 1979).

Despite the relatively straightforward technical nature of the task involved, the experience of highways agency has none the less proved a major source of irritation to most MCC surveyors. As the County Surveyor of West Midlands MCC put it:

If we followed the logic of our argument and if we had the political will, we would withdraw agency, but unless we could be sure the district councils would give up claiming powers, it would not be worth withdrawing.

(Interview, July 1984)

In most of the metropolitan areas, attempts were made sooner or later to clawback highways agency powers. South Yorkshire did so after only two years in 1976, at the cost of considerable inter-tier contention and with the result that all four of its districts claimed the right to maintain urban unclassified roads under Section 187 of the 1972 Act. West Midlands renegotiated the highways agency agreement with their districts in 1979 (excluding Birmingham, as did Tyne and Wear in 1981. Greater Manchester was treading the same path with considerable determination in 1982 with a new County Engineer who had direct experience of the arrangements in West Yorkshire, when the need to maintain good relations with the district councils in the light of the government's abolition proposal became a more important consideration. The proposed renegotiation was cancelled.

The main point to stress is that political response to pressure from the new, aggrieved districts (who stood to lose all highways powers in 1972–3) led to a dilution of the MCCs' highways responsibilities, which in the view of most county engineers limited the ability of the county council to implement a 'fair' distribution of highways maintenance investment, in relation to the different needs of the different parts of the county. It also proved frustrating in that it denied the MCCs the opportunity of showing how economically and efficiently they could run the service if it had been solely their responsibility. The agency arrangements inevitably generated overlap and duplication, as both tiers concerned themselves with the same set of schemes (see Flynn, 1984). Finally, highways provided the basis for some of the county–district conflicts, which (apparently) weighed so heavily with the government in deciding that change was necessary.

The Metropolitan County Councils as Providers of Services

Whatever else may be said about the strategic role of the MCCs, in the terms we have defined it has not been a particularly costly operation. The numbers of staff employed are small, and costs per head are equivalent (in planning at least) to those in the shire counties (see Appendix 3). In other areas of activity, however, particularly the direct provision of services, and to a lesser extent (in the MCCs) the interventionist role, there is more of a case to answer. One of the government's stated reasons for disbanding the GLC and the MCCs is that they are viewed as spending too much, either as a result of the promotion of (expensive) policies which conflict with national policies (for example, passenger transport fares subsidization) and/or because they are wasteful or inefficient. In *Streamlining the Cities* it is argued that the MCCs as a group have 'consistently exceeded the expenditure targets set for them by central government' and have 'increased their expenditure significantly more than other local authorities in England' (para. 1.13). The average cash increase between 1978/9 and 1983/4, in terms of net current expenditure budgeted for has, it is claimed, been 111 per cent in the metropolitan counties as compared with 80 per cent for other local authorities in England (excluding the GLC whose equivalent figure has been 127 per cent!). In volume terms these figures imply expenditure increases of 22 per cent for the MCCs as compared with 4 per cent for other local authorities – again excluding the GLC (paras 1.14 and 1.15).

It is accepted by the government (para. 1.15) that some of the differences in these figures can be accounted for by the priority which the government itself has given to the law and order services. If police expenditure is excluded, however, it is claimed that the metropolitan counties as a group increased expenditure in volume terms (that is, in terms of the value of the volume of goods and services purchased by the MCCs) between 1978 and 1983 by 12 per cent as compared with a standstill position in other authorities in England (excluding the GLC). While emphasizing at the outset that higher per capita expenditure in one type of authority does not necessarily imply 'wastefulness' or 'inefficiency' it is useful to examine, using the most recent CIPFA statistics on Local Government Expenditure (1984), how MCCs compare in this respect with authorities carrying out similar functions. Appendix 3 sets out comparisons that can appropriately be made and confirms that MCCs do indeed spend more per capita on most of the services for which they are responsible than do shire counties (although it should be noted that in relation to trading standards for which London boroughs are responsible, the borough figure is well above that of the metropolitan counties). This general finding does however hide significant differences among the MCCs themselves. Using CIPFA statistics it is possible to compare per capita expenditure for the above range of services and public transport across the six metropolitan counties (see Appendix 4).

These figures also show significant disparities in all the services concerned. The variations in leisure and recreation expenditure reflect the different involvement of different MCCs in this field, particularly with regard to museums and art galleries. Expenditure is high in Tyne and Wear and Merseyside (and to a lesser extent in South Yorkshire) and negligible elsewhere. In the light of the considerable variations around the average which Bristow *et al.*'s (1984) figures show, it is clear that by no means all the MCCs have higher than average (*vis-à-vis* all authorities providing such services) per capita expenditure on all the relevant functions. Indeed in the case of Greater Manchester and West Midlands County Council, per capita expenditure in 1983/4 was well below the metropolitan county average. If 'excessive expenditure' is a major criteria in the abolition argument, it seems abolition should be a much more selective process!

However, there are a number of reasons why one authority may spend more than another on its range of services, only one of which is that it is inefficient. Coopers and Lybrand in their first report for the metropolitan counties on *Streamlining the Cities* (Coopers and Lybrand Associates, 1983) make this argument powerfully and examine the figures quoted by the government (see pp. 86–7 above) in this light. Coopers and Lybrand argue as follows:

> Judgements about expenditure without proper consideration of the factors behind it can be misleading. Setting the level of a local authority's expenditure is part of a complex process. This process involves an authority in the identification of the relevant needs of its area; to meet these needs it seeks to develop effective policies for its services and then to find efficient ways of implementing them. The level of expenditure is a function of all these three factors.

Coopers and Lybrand go on to show that if one takes the government's figures for the discrepancy in volume change in expenditure between 1978/9 and 1983/4 (13 per cent for metropolitan counties; 1·5 per cent for other authorities) and adjusts for the fact that the government's own expectations of volume change over the period vary from service to service, then the gap lessens. The government's own plans for local authority service volume change, as measured by the figures it accepts as eligible for rate support grant, anticipated greater growth in expenditure on police and fire than most other services, and the metropolitan counties expenditure profile is disproportionately dominated by these two functions as Appendix 2 shows. Inflation has also been running above average in these services due to nationally negotiated pay settlements. The survey further concludes that for police, fire and highways, there are factors associated with need which explain some of the higher levels of expenditure. For public transport, available evidence from independent studies indicates that policy decisions made by the MCCs have been on a sound financial basis (in that for each £1 of subsidy, economic benefits of £1·20–£1·30 were produced in four of the MCCs; in South Yorkshire the latter figure was around £1). Also their passenger transport undertakings are generally as efficient as those of other operators (ibid., p. 18). Differences in levels of expenditure are a reflection of the application of political judgement as to the most appropriate response to need, *not* a reflection of waste and inefficiency.

Streamlining the Cities points out that between 1981/2 and April 1983, MCC precept levels increased by 29 per cent whereas the general rate poundage for all English authorities (including the MCCs and the GLC) increased by only 20 per cent. One of the major factors governing the level of the MCC precept is, of course, the amount of block grant (and specific grant) received, or which it is expected will be received. The overall amount of block grant made available by the government is distributed between individual authorities primarily on the basis of Grant Related Expenditure Assessments (GREAs). The Coopers and Lybrand report concludes that the approaches now used to the GREAs for local transport, concessionary fares and waste disposal produce a bias against the MCCs compared with other types of English local authorities. The report points out that one major consequence of the fact that GREAs do not represent need effectively is that the MCCs receive proportionately less grant for their expenditure than other authorities. This effect is reinforced by the relatively higher spending of the MCCs (for the reasons discussed above) and the penalties imposed (by withholding grant) for breaching government targets. The report is of the view that

> There is no doubt that the imposition of target penalties was a major contributor to the higher increase in MCCs precept levels, as high spenders were penalised much more severely in 1983/84 than they were in 1981/82.
>
> (ibid., p. 24)

The general conclusions of the study by a firm of consultants – which the present government itself has used for a number of commissions – throw a good deal of doubt on the arguments made in the White Paper about the wastefulness of MCCs. There are good reasons – differential inflation, government advice, level of need and the justifiable exercise of local political choice – which account for most of the discrepancy in the volume growth of MCC expenditure, *vis-à-vis* that of other English authorities. Also the difference in precept levels referred to is largely explained by changes in the grant aid target penalty system and the different uses made of balances in the MCCs (compared with elsewhere). One of the most worrying aspects of the debate over the future of the MCCs is the failure of the government to produce a reasoned response to the substantiated arguments put forward in the Coopers and Lybrand report. Little has been done other than to reassert the figures quoted in the White Paper.

It is worth recalling some of the problems of service delivery which the creation of the MCCs in 1973 was specifically aimed at countering. The arrangements for waste disposal in the metropolitan areas were widely considered to be unsatisfactory (see Redcliffe-Maud, 1969). Many districts, having almost run out of surface tips, had been obliged to invest in the much less cost-effective method of incineration. Treatment of waste disposal over a much wider area has in principle overcome most of these localized problems, although ironically the narrow definition of some of the MCCs (especially the West Midlands) has meant that they are having to look outside existing boundaries in their attempts to carry out this function. The consistency of the application of trading standards and the quality of consumer protection services had varied considerably from district to district before 1974. The allocation of this responsibility to the MCCs has overcome this problem. Indeed the Confederation of British Industry (CBI, 1983) has expressed considerable concern about the implications of the loss in this consistency of the trading standard services across metropolitan areas. The confusing pattern of a largely district- or borough-provided public transport system which existed in the conurbations in the 1960s was a major reason for the setting up of the PTA/PTE system in 1968 and the allocation of that function to the MCCs in 1974. The provision in the White Paper for 'individual districts to provide separate services and to enter into contractual arrangements with other operators in the public or private sectors' provides an opportunity for reintroduction of the confusion which led to the legislation in 1968 and 1972.

The Performance of the Interventionist Role

In the MCCs the interventionist role has been developed to a certain extent (and certainly beyond anything contemplated in the MCCs before 1981). However, the process has been altogether a more limited and less publicized one than in London. There has certainly been in each MCC a commitment to tackling the economic problems of their areas. There has been a certain amount of funding of voluntary groups, though on nothing like the same scale as in the GLC. However, comments on foreign policy and the establishment of women's and race committees have been much less common. Indeed the political views of most of the MCC leaders would generally be regarded as more moderate than those of the leaders of many of the Labour-controlled districts (for example, Sheffield, Liverpool, Manchester and several of the London boroughs).

In each metropolitan area the economic base has become severely eroded since the mid-1970s. On Merseyside and in Tyne and Wear, economic decline and a high and increasing level of unemployment had become established trends well before then. In the late 1970s the four other metropolitan areas suffered sharp declines in manufacturing output and employment, the hitherto prosperous West Midlands being particularly severely hit. It is hardly surprising therefore that the economic development role has been enthusiastically pursued since 1981 by all metropolitan counties. This activity could have been pursued in a strategic way (a detailed analysis of the problems and potential of different industrial sectors within the metropolitan area; the development of sector- and location-based strategy to overcome problems and exploit potential; and the allocation of resources on this basis). However, although the GLC and, to a lesser extent, West Midlands have been moving in this direction, the economic development activity has not generally been pursued in this way in the metropolitan counties. The process has been more one of opportunism and reaction to crisis. The Enterprise Boards which have been set up in one form or another by all the MCCs have tended to come to the aid of small and medium-sized firms in financial difficulties (so long as certain criteria, for example in relation to employers' attitudes to the workforce and to trade unionism, have been met) as and when such crises have occurred, and they have been approached by the firms in question. They have also favoured and tried to encourage socialist forms of enterprise (for example, workers' co-ops). Hence, although there has been a pattern for the distribution of aid in terms of type of company, it is likely that in terms of locational distribution, any relative benefit to one sub-area rather than another has been accidental rather than planned.

It is likely that it is this kind of activity that the government has in mind when referring to 'the search for a wider role [which] brings them [the metropolitan counties] into conflict with the lower-tier authorities. It may also lead them to promote policies which conflict with national policies which are the responsibility of central government.' If this is true, then the conflict between the metropolitan counties and the government has been a much more significant factor than any conflict (on these topics) between counties and districts. Apart from some demarcation disputes over economic development in the Liverpool Inner City Partnership, economic development has not been a major issue of inter-tier contention. In most metropolitan areas problems of economic decline and unemployment are so serious that districts are glad to see any investment, aid or infrastructure provision within their boundaries whoever provides it.

Thus, as in the GLC case, the figures for expenditure on services such as economic development do not demonstrate that the MCCs are wasteful or are spending unnecessarily. What they do reflect are differences in value judgements about the overall policies of such authorities. In the White Paper technical arguments about efficiency and economy mask profound ideological differences between central and local government about the proper response to a range of issues including economic decline. It is not that the present government does not wish to see local authorities taking action over economic decline. Indeed, four of the MCCs contain an inner city partnership. (Manchester/Salford, Liverpool, Newcastle/Gateshead, Birmingham) and all contain at least one programme authority. In each case the government approves and funds (on a 75 per cent basis) a programme largely devoted to the provision of infrastructure, aid and environmental improvement, as a catalyst to economic regeneration. However, it is clear that central government has become seriously concerned about the alternative conceptions of economic policy espoused by the metropolitan counties and the GLC, and the use of Section 137 powers which have resulted. The government has clearly also been unhappy about the attitude of all the MCCs to civil defence (that is, their refusal to co-operate with Home Office exercises purporting to simulate post-nuclear-attack conditions and their declaration of nuclear-free zones) and of attempts by some to aid MDCs in the provision of welfare rights advice facilities.

The issue of Section 137 powers merits further comment. The CBI proposals (CBI, 1983) for the reform of local government in metropolitan areas objected to the use of discretionary power to spend the product of a 2p rate on any matter of benefit to the people of the area. This power was contained in Section 137 of the Local Government Act 1972. However, the expenditure made under this power does not show disproportionate use by MCCs seeking a role for themselves. Crawford and Moore (1983) show that the GLC and the MCCs together spent £8·5 million under this power in 1981/2 out of a total expenditure by all authorities of £28·6 million. The metropolitan district councils and London boroughs spent £9·2 million alone (p. 87). They also show that the GLC and MCCs spent the same proportion of the available Section 137 money as the London boroughs and MDCs, at 10·76 per cent (p. 90). Since 1981 the GLC and the MCCs have attempted to increase their Section 137 expenditure.

Accountability of the MCCs

The MCCs, it is suggested in *Streamlining the Cities*, are remote, inaccessible and little understood by the public (paras 1.9 and 1.11). As with so much of the content of the White Paper, this view is not supported by any evidence. There is, in fact, little evidence to support it. Although comprehensive voting turnout figures are not available in published form, Bristow (1978, p. 21) shows that the voting turnout in 1973 was 37 per cent in metropolitan counties compared with 34 per cent at metropolitan district level; and in 1976/7 the comparative figures were 41 per cent and 38 per cent. In the Greater London Council voting turnout has risen from 37 per cent (1973) to 43 per cent (1977) to 44 per cent (1981) and compares favourably with London borough voting turnouts in adjacent years. There is thus no case to be made that voters perceived MCCs (and the GLC) as being less politically significant, as assessed by voting turnout.

There are a number of public opinion surveys which show that people living in metropolitan areas (and elsewhere) are often confused about the distribution of functions between county and district (and indeed between local government and other agencies – see MORI, 1980, for the London Borough of Southwark, Kenny and McEvoy, 1980; 1983). Such confusion does not however reflect on peoples' views of metropolitan counties *per se*; it reflects on districts as much as counties and gives no more basis for abolishing one level than the other.

Recent public opinion polls also demonstrate majorities in favour of the retention of the MCCs as opposed to their abolition. Whereas the indications are that the MCCs were not particularly well understood or appreciated organizations in the first few years of their existence (partly reflecting their newness and their precepting – versus direct rating – role), it does seem that the heightened awareness of their existence generated since the publication of the government's abolition proposals has resulted in many members of the public changing their views. Faced with the alternatives – more central government control, creation of a panoply of joint boards – the MCCs do not perhaps seem quite so remote and inaccessible!

Co-operation and Conflict Within the Metropolitan Counties

The poor quality of relationships in the two-tier system of metropolitan government has ostensibly been one of the major concerns of central government in advocating change. *Streamlining the Cities* contains the following statement:

The 1960's and early 1970's were also the heyday of a certain fashion for strategic planning, the confidence in which now appears exaggerated ... in this situation the GLC and the MCCs have found it difficult to establish a role for themselves ... the search for a wider role brings them into conflict with the lower-tier authorities. (para. 1.3)

and later

Abolition will remove a source of conflict and tension. (para. 1.19)

These assertions give rise to three important questions. First, how widespread really is this 'conflict and tension' in metropolitan areas? Secondly, what are the major causes of conflict? Thirdly, over what issues does conflict arise (conflicts of interest or inter-organizational rivalry)? In Chapter 1 it was argued that any system of government needs to allow interest conflicts to be acted out and resolved either within or between institutions.

The recently completed SSRC research project on the two-tier system in England (see Introduction) is the major source of evidence used in addressing these questions. In the research a distinction was made between co-operative and confluctual relationships and relationships best categorized as 'neutral' where differences of view or interest simmered below the surface without necessarily becoming overt.

It was discovered in our research, in line with the findings of DeGrove (1977), Dixon (1978) and Alexander (1982) that there is indeed a certain amount of conflict to be found in relationships between MCCs and MDCs and between the GLC and London boroughs (see Young and Kramer, 1978; Wistrich, 1972). It would indeed be surprising if this were not the case. Conflict was also to be found in relationships in the old pre-1974 two-tier system (see Lee *et al.*, 1974; Richards, 1956) and it occurs in several circumstances in relationships between water authorities and local authorities (see Stafford, 1983) and between health authorities and local authorities (see Webb and Wistow, 1983). It is indeed a common feature in inter-authority relationships generally.

One of the exercises carried out in our research was to map the whole range of county–district relationships between West Midlands and three of its boroughs (Solihull, Sandwell, Birmingham) and between the GLC and four of its boroughs (Barnet, Brent, Harrow, Tower Hamlets). Any relationship between a county and a district consists, of course, of a number of different strands (for example, waste collection, waste disposal, consultations over the TPP, highways agency, strategic planning applications) which often operate in very different ways. The mapping exercise indicated for each strand, the quality of relationship (co-operative/neutral/

manifest conflict) the extent to which it had changed over previous years and a number of other features (for example, degree of formality, degree of intensity).

The main conclusion was clear. Co-existing with periodic outbreaks of overt conflict, or longer periods of attrition in connection with particular shared or contingent functions, there was found in all examples studied a much larger set of such functions which were proceeding in a co-operative or, at the very least, a neutral way. Most of the time in relation to most functions, the relationship of the metropolitan counties with their districts is not a recipe for conflict and uncertainty.

This was true even in those relationships which by reputation have been the most contentious. With regard to Birmingham/West Midlands and Solihull/West Midlands, for most areas of interaction, most of the time relationships were co-operative or neutral. Conflict has been the exception rather than the rule and, when it has occurred, has not always lasted very long. The use of the term 'conflict' to describe the overall relationship between metropolitan counties (and the GLC) and their districts would be grossly misleading – even in the two cases mentioned. Indeed in all the metropolitan counties, the conflicts which have been found have been underlaid by a large area of relatively uncontentious activity (with the possible exception of West Yorkshire: see Dixon, 1978) in its first three or four years, and West Midlands during the same period.

It was also apparent from interviews carried out by us in other metropolitan areas, and from other work done, that the quality of relationships (within the above general pattern) has varied within and between different metropolitan areas. Relations in Tyne and Wear have been relatively consensual, reflecting the uniform Labour Party control of county and (with one exception, for a short time) all districts since 1974. Greater Manchester and its districts have enjoyed a reasonable relationship for most of the decade, soured recently by a county attempt to clawback highways agency and the political opportunism of one or two Conservative leaders. Indeed the joint actions between Greater Manchester and various combinations of the MDCs in the schemes for the improvement of river valleys is a good example of the positive co-operation which can result, if the circumstances are appropriate (see Maund, 1982). On Merseyside the relationship betwen the county and Liverpool has always been difficult, at least for as long as the minority Liberal administration was in power in the City (see for example, House of Commons, Environment Committee, 1983). There had also been persistent problems with Sefton. On the other hand, relationships with St Helens and, until very recently, Knowsley have been good and co-operation with Wirral, especially over the Inner Area

Programme, was prevalent until the relatively recent polarization of political control between the two authorities.

In South Yorkshire political jealousies following loss of county borough status in 1974 caused tension between Sheffield MDC and the county council especially over the Dearne Valley priority in the county structure plan (see Darke, 1980); all the districts objected strongly to the withdrawal of highways agency responsibilities from 1976 onwards. Otherwise the common political orientation, as in Tyne and Wear, has been an integrative force, especially recently. In West Midlands there were difficulties right from the start, reflecting concern over lost county borough status (in one case only recently acquired) and particularly marked in relation to Birmingham and Solihull. Dudley/West Midlands proved the most co-operative relationship until recently. In West Yorkshire political rivalries again caused immense problems in the first three years. Relationships had, however, improved significantly since that date, particularly in land-use planning. Nowhere in the MCCs, however, has the strength of inter-tier political linkages, apparent between certain Labour-controlled London boroughs and the GLC (see Chapter 3) been replicated.

Overall, county–district relationships in metropolitan areas have deteriorated somewhat since 1981, although by no means uniformly due to the polarization of political views within many of these areas, with 'new right' Conservative-controlled district councils initiating since 1981 pressure for the abolition of the metropolitan counties (Birmingham/West Midlands; Trafford/Greater Manchester; Sefton/Merseyside, plus several examples in London). There is no evidence that it has reflected increasing problems of operating services for which there is shared or contingent responsibilities; rather difference in political ideology has been a far more telling factor.

The Nature of Inter-Tier Conflict

In any system of government in which interrelated powers are distributed between different agencies, the potential for conflict exists. Metropolitan counties and districts are linked together in a number of different ways (though not in as rich and complex a way as shire counties and districts are linked). They share a concern with and some responsibility for *inter alia* the rates, roads, planning, waste processing, economic development and recreation and the arts. All these shared or linked responsibilities represent potentialities for the generation of different views (based on political, professional or territorial differences) and a channel for the expression of such views. Under certain circumstances, the significance of these differences and the difficulty of resolving them may result in overt conflict.

It is important to distinguish between three different types of conflicts in such relations: symbolic conflict; substantive (policy) conflict; and procedural/technical conflict. Symbolic conflict refers to the fact that there are some actions undertaken by the county, which although a district may strongly disapprove of them and publicly register that disapproval, it can, in effect, do little about them. Thus if a county imposes a precept which represents a significant increase on the previous year's precept (or, when they were legally empowered to do so, a supplementary precept) then a district, however much it might disagree with the need for it, has little choice but to collect it on behalf of the county. Opposition to school closures is a further case in point in shire counties. Conflict in these circumstances is symbolic; it provides an outlet for political differences without affecting the outcome of the issue. The only recourse a district has in relation to a responsibility which is solely that of the county is to challenge it in the courts; a gambit extremely uncommon until recently but successfully used by Bromley in relation to the GLC's Fares Fair policy in 1982 and by Solihull in relation to West Midlands fares reduction policy in the same year.

Substantive or policy conflict refers to quite legitimate differences of view about the best course of action in a service for which both tiers have some kind of responsibility; economic development, the content of a local plan; the allocation of highways maintenance budget, and so on. The outcome in this case reflects the differential bargaining powers of the two parties and the success of the strategy/ tactics deployed. One of the problems in the current system is that it contains a number of 'grey areas' in the division of powers and responsibilities where who does what is by no means clear. This is particularly true, although less so now that it was before 1980, of the world of land-use planning and also applies to a lesser extent to the activities of highways maintenance and economic development. The existence of such 'grey areas' provides an opportunity for the third type of conflict – that which revolves around issues of procedure and technical detail. The wider these 'grey areas' the more potential there is for conflicts of policy to spill over into attempts to exploit unclear technical or procedural criteria to further one's position. Thus, if legitimate differences of opinion are superimposed on lack of clarity of responsibility then one does have a recipe for uncertainty, delay and frustration. This situation does not in itself of course suggest that one or other tier should be abolished. A tidying-up operation, clarifying the powers available to each tier is a perfectly feasible alternative. This approach has been tried, with apparent success in

Scotland, since the publication of the Stodart Report (1982) and subsequent legislation.

Conflict may represent differences in political interests or differences in bureaucratic interests (or in certain circumstances a combination of both). Some of the conflict in MCCs which we discovered in our research was clearly bureaucratic in origin, and reflected differences of professional opinion (both within and between professions) or battles over domain (that is, attempts typically made by bureaucracies to carve out areas of responsibility which are exclusively or predominantly their own). This familiar area of administrative politics underlaid many of the conflicts over highway agency agreements, and the exercise of the (somewhat unclear) planning legislation prior to 1980. However, other examples of conflict reflected differences in political interest. Such political differences could be territorially based (for example, the choice of areas outside Sheffield as priority areas in the South Yorkshire Structure Plan) or class-based (for example, the opposition by Solihull MDC to the attempt by West Midlands to introduce a 'cheap fares' policy in 1982, which would have predominantly benefited working-class public transport users living outside Solihull at significant cost to middle-class ratepayers living inside the borough). Clashes of political interest are more likely to occur at the symbolic or substantive level; clashes of bureaucratic interest at the substantive or procedural/technical level. In general, as we have seen, inter-tier conflicts based on a difference of class interests have been relatively few and far between within the MCCs.

If the level of conflict, such as it is, within metropolitan counties is a major reason for changing the system, there would be a good case for change in several other parts of the country. Some earlier Institute of Local Government Studies (INLOGOV) research on the two-tier system (INLOGOV, 1977) showed that, on the basis of a number of attitudinal criteria, tensions were as great within several shire counties as in the metropolitan areas (INLOGOV, 1977). Conflict was particularly prevalent between many of the large ex-county boroughs in shire counties (which had lost powers in 1974 much more spectacularly than had the ex-county boroughs in the metropolitan areas) and the counties in which they found themselves. These tensions flared up again at the time of the previous Labour government's *Organic Change* proposals (see Stewart, Leach and Skelcher, 1979) and have in many such areas simmered away since.

The Pattern of Conflict: An Analysis by Service

The areas of contention in metropolitan counties have been less wide-ranging than is commonly imagined. The interface between waste collection (a district responsibility) and waste disposal (a county responsibility) has, for example, been largely unproblematical, with the occasional early dispute over ownership of assets and a few MDC complaints about length of journey to tip providing the only minor examples of tension. Similarly, although some Conservative-controlled districts do not approve of the Enterprise Boards set up by metropolitan counties, there have been few who-does-what issues in economic development apart from the Liverpool/Merseyside 'lead-role' dispute (see House of Commons, Environment Committee Report, 1982–3) and a minor version of the same issue in Birmingham/West Midlands (ibid.). Apart from in West Yorkshire where there was a long and ultimately unsuccessful attempt by the county to carve out a role in the leisure and recreation field (see Dixon, 1978, pp. 98 ff.), the other metropolitan counties and districts worked out before April 1974 an acceptable distribution of responsibilities, sometimes involving the county with a major role in this field (Merseyside, Tyne and Wear), sometimes with a relatively minor one (Greater Manchester, West Midlands). Occasional 'who should fund what' disagreements have been the only ripples of dissension here (with the exception of the role of the county structure plan – see above). Potential disputes over the Community Land Act were soon minimized by the advent of a period of Conservative control in most metropolitan counties and many metropolitan districts from around 1976/7. Apart from Liverpool, county–district relationships in the various inner city partnerships and programmes have often been co-operative (Wolverhampton, Wirral, Newcastle) or at worst neutral (Sheffield, Birmingham, Bolton).

Apart from 'symbolic' conflicts occasionally leading to court cases, over public transport subsidies and precept levels of the MCCs, and the wide-ranging set of conflicts over all manner of matters in West Yorkshire between 1974 and 1977 (see Dixon, 1978, pp. 59 ff.), this leaves two major areas of contention: land-use planning and highways agency.

As discussed earlier, there has been a degree of inter-tier conflict in land-use planning as the metropolitan counties have tried to put the concept of a 'strategic role' into operation. It would have been surprising if this had not been the case. Indeed the lack of such conflict would have weakened rather than strengthened the argument for a metropolitan-wide strategic land-use planning role. It is hardly surprising that counties and districts should differ over structure plan provisions or Green Belt definition or particular planning decisions (for example, whether or not to allow a hypermarket in a particular location). Indeed, as we have argued in Chapter 1 there is virtue in a system which allows conflicting political interests (class or territory based) to be expressed. The problem in land-use planning has been that the rather vague (until 1980) division of responsibilities left ample scope for legitimate differences of political interest over substantive policy to become channelled into bureaucratic disputes over procedure and 'who-does-what'. These disputes were minimized by the relatively low-key approach to the implementation of the strategic role adopted in most metropolitan counties, but they have surfaced from time to time in all areas over issues such as alleged use of the structure plan as a means of entry into areas of district responsibility (West Yorkshire, Greater Manchester, West Midlands); alleged involvement of counties in detail of applications which should be of district concern only (all counties; with the role of the county engineers in this respect being as much a bone of contention as the county planning officer); particularly contentious policies in the structure plan (South Yorkshire, Greater Manchester), ownership of local plans (for example, Greater Manchester River Valleys); and the alleged non-conformity of local plans with county strategy (Greater Manchester/Bolton; West Yorkshire/Leeds; Tyne and Wear/Newcastle). It should be noted that the lack of such disputes is not necessarily a sign that the system is working well.

These conflicts have much more frequently involved differences of bureaucratic interest or professional perception than they have differences in political interests (although politicians have often been brought into the arena by the officers involved). Indeed, political input to land-use planning in MCCs was of a fairly low-key nature until after 1981. By this time, conflicts in all MCCs had become less common anyway reflecting the further limitation of the county council's strategic role embodied in the Local Government Planning and Land Act 1980.

The problems of highways agency have also already been discussed to some extent. These have operated at two levels: first, periodic small-scale detailed disputes over the interpretation of the terms of the agency agreement (level of allocation; reimbursement of administrative costs; efficiency of use of staff and materials by districts; who does what in times of crisis, for example, heavy snowfall) and secondly, disputes around the renegotiation or withdrawal of the agency agreement. The former which have mostly involved differences of bureaucratic interest have been prevalent in all metropolitan counties and are probably hard to avoid in an agency type of system. They have perhaps been least apparent in Merseyside and Tyne and Wear. More significant in conflict terms have been the attempts by metropolitan counties to withdraw or radically negotiate highways agency in West Midlands (in 1979), South Yorkshire (in 1976) and Greater Manchester (in 1982). These have reflected differences of both political (territorial) interest and interdepartmental domain disputes. The conflict in West Midlands was centred particularly on Birmingham, with disputes over winter gritting and responsibility for inner ring road repairs featuring strongly (see Hughes, 1979, pp. 182–92). South Yorkshire's withdrawal of agency left a legacy of bad feeling amongst districts, whereas Greater Manchester's attempt was overtaken by considerations of survival, and prudently dropped (or shelved), having however already generated a lot of resistance from districts. In this field at least, West Yorkshire has avoided the problems of the other metropolitan counties.

Conclusion: The Functions of Inter-tier Conflict

What, then, is to be concluded about the nature of county–district relations in metropolitan areas, and what are the implications for the current move to abolish the GLC and the metropolitan counties? First, conflict has been patchy rather than widespread. The picture painted by *Streamlining the Cities* is misleading. The division of functions between MCCs and MDCs has not been a recipe for conflict and uncertainty. It has created problems and conflicts at the interface, as any system of shared or contingent responsibilities will. However, in our view, the degree of conflict in inter-tier relationships in metropolitan areas has been seriously over-emphasized.

The second point to emphasize is that class-based and territorial-based conflict is only to be expected within metropolitan areas, and a system which allows such conflicts to be expressed and resolved is arguably to be commended. There is an inherent tension in metropolitan areas between their unity in the economic sphere and their diversity in the social sphere. Differences of view and more importantly of class interest exist throughout our society and are manifested in differences over what policies should be pursued, in what areas and at what cost. These differences emerge within and between local authorities and the metropolitan areas have been one arena where this has inevitably happened. The Regional Studies Association in its response to *Streamlining the Cities* (RSA, 1984, p. 14) puts the point:

Is the described conflict of interest between metropolitan government and the tiers of government above and below a legitimate one, symptomatic of a genuine and valid constituency of opinion which deserves a role in our society, and hence a democratic voice? If the answer is yes, then one must ask what effect abolition of the present democratic forum at city regional level might have in such policy debates?

The School for Advanced Urban Studies (SAUS, 1983, p. 9) argues that the White Paper 'fails to recognise that metropolitan governments are designed as vehicles for the resolution of conflicts and tensions that inevitably occur between smaller territorial units of government'. A strategic planning authority that did not periodically come into conflict with its lower-tier units would not be doing its job properly.

Thirdly, there is the question of who or what is responsible for the 'conflict' within metropolitan areas. To some extent, as we have shown, the lack of clarity with which functions have been distributed between the tiers has left various 'grey areas' which have been open to exploitation, in conflict terms, for those wishing to do so. One response to this situation is of course to clarify the distribution of powers as happened in Scotland, following the publication of the Stodart Report in 1981. Inter-tier conflict in Scotland is currently at a relatively low level (see Leach, Flynn and Vielba, 1985). However, the government has paid little attention to the arguments of the Stodart Report or their implementation in its current proposals.

The issue remains of who has had the primary responsibility for exploiting the areas of potential conflict, particularly those who offer opportunities for substantive (policy) conflict to spill over into technical and procedural arguments. In one sense, of course, the answer must be that both tiers are responsible: it takes two to generate a conflict. However, if one probes a little deeper, a number of important differences emerge in the powers and bargaining positions possessed by the different tiers. The government is right to recognize that 'in the metropolitan areas, the boroughs and district councils are the primary local government units. They are responsible for the majority of local spending' (DoE, 1983, para. 1.9). Others have argued in similar vein that, unlike the situation in shire counties, the balance of power in metropolitan areas lies with the districts (Alexander, 1982, p. 38; Leach and Moore, 1979, p. 174).

In addition, in 1974 most of the metropolitan districts were based upon existing county boroughs, with a resulting continuity of knowledge and experience at both officer and councillor level, whereas the metropolitan counties were new entities starting from scratch in both respects. It was bound to take time for these new units to establish themselves. In trying to do so it is hardly surprising that some of them did things which in retrospect could be judged as tactical errors (for example, West Yorkshire's attempt to establish a major recreational role: Dixon, 1978, pp. 98 ff.; South Yorkshire's withdrawal of highways agency in 1976).

What is apparent from Dixon's study, Alexander's research (1982), our own work, and a number of other studies (DeGrove, 1977, p. 4), is that the stance towards the new county of many of the new metropolitan districts, particularly the large cities with long and proud civic traditions, reflected directly their concern over lost status. In some cases the attitudes of an aggrieved chief executive were clearly the main motive force (see Dixon, 1978, pp. 76–9). It was much more common, however, for important local councillors to feel and express most strongly such resentment. The problem that metropolitan counties had in establishing an identifiable and internally unifying role was clearly aggravated in many instances by the desire of aggrieved actors in the new metropolitan districts to demonstrate the unworkability of and lack of necessity for the new system. If much of the county–district conflict in metropolitan areas has its roots in such feelings of disgruntlement and status loss, then it seems more than a little misleading and unjust to imply that the main cause of conflict is 'the search for a wider role' on the part of the metropolitan counties.

The government's condemnation of the GLC and the MCCs for attempting to play a strategic role of one kind or another is a little strange when this is one of the express purposes for which they were designed in 1972! One of the problems for the MCCs since 1974, and particularly since 1980, is that the powers to implement this strategic role effectively have not been available, their boundaries have been inappropriate, and the strategic problems have changed. A number of those commenting on the White Paper's arguments have emphasized that the need for a strategic city-region-wide role is as strong as it ever was (see RSA, 1984, p. 11; SAUS, 1984, p. 9; Greater London Group, 1984, p. 10). To regard strategic planning as a 'certain fashion' prevalent in the 1960s and 1970s 'the confidence in which now appears exaggerated' is to misunderstand the nature of strategic planning. The need for strategic planning is in fact tacitly acknowledged at several points in the White Paper (see for example paras 2.5–2.7). The implication must again be drawn (see also Chapter 1) that it is the government who wishes to extend its own strategic role in the metropolitan areas. The districts acting in conjunction are extremely unlikely to be capable of such a role; and successive consultation documents issued in connection with the land-use planning function have implied an ever more important DoE role.

The case for the provision of services such as police, fire, public transport and trading standards over an area much wider than that of the existing metropolitan district, on the basis both of 'economies of scale' and/or 'the nature of the problem addressed' is as strong as it was when Redcliffe-Maud, after three years of detailed consideration, made it in 1969. The argument made in the White Paper that the MCCs are less efficient organizations than other local authorities is not justified from the evidence available. The need for strategic planning of one kind or another at something approximating to the metropolitan level is widely acknowledged. The need for a democratically elected resource-allocation body, intermediate between central government and district/borough authorities has been well argued by a number of different writers (for example, Marshall, 1978, pp. 94–6). Thus, while the current form of metropolitan government may leave a lot to be desired, the case for some form of 'city regional' authority is still a strong one as we shall see in Chapter 5.

5 The Future of Metropolitan Government

> I've always said that if abolition does not save money, I
> will consider that the government has failed. But there will
> be savings. There will be savings resulting from policy
> changes.
>
> (Patrick Jenkin at a meeting with three members of
> Merseyside NALGO, 13 July 1984)

Is There a Need for Reform?

The MCCs have gained few friends since their establishment. The
Local Government Act which established them was very different
from the Labour Party's proposed local government reform and the
proposals of the preceding Royal Commission in that MCCs were
established in different places, with different functions. Where they
were established in the same general areas as those contained in the
Labour White Paper, the boundaries were drawn more tightly around
the urban areas. The Labour Party has never been strongly
committed to the post-1974 local government system. As we have
seen the Conservative Party has been unhappy with the recent
development of the MCCs and their policy stances, and has been
concerned that all the MCCs have recently been under Labour
control. The Social Democratic and Liberal parties are in favour of
regional government, which they say would preclude the existence of
an intermediate tier between a regional level of government and the
basic units of local government.

As we have seen, the distribution of functions, both in the Greater
London area and in the metropolitan counties, has made the task of
the upper-tier authorities difficult. The division of the planning
function between the tiers has made the strategic land-use function
weak through the paucity of implementation powers. The reduction
of the GLC housing role and the failure to give the MCCs the housing
policy powers recommended by Redcliffe-Maud, together with the
decision to give education to the MDCs and not the MCCs, meant
that the upper tier had control of none of the main social policy
instruments. In most cases the MCC boundaries were drawn too close
to the edges of conurbations to allow strategic planning or resource

allocation which took account of the nature of the patterns of development, the growing suburbs being mainly outside.

The flawed design of the local government system, particularly in the metropolitan areas, has allowed many district councils to argue that they should be single-tier, 'most-purpose' authorities. They have made the case that there are very few functions which need to be carried out on a scale greater than that of the district council, and that those which need a wider boundary could be carried out through some form of co-operation. The same argument has been applied in the case of London. The counter case, that the MCCs and the GLC should be strengthened by an extension of powers, or by a development of a resource allocation role, has made little ground since the losers in such a reallocation of powers would be the district and borough councils.

Hence a reform of the system in the metropolitan areas was likely, whichever party was in government. The timing of the reform depended on the particular political circumstances, as we saw in Chapter 1. A question which remains is, should the reform be limited to the metropolitan areas? *Streamlining the Cities* simply says that since the shire county councils provide services which account for 87 per cent of the services in their areas, they are doing a worthwhile job and reform is not needed (para. 1.8). Reform in the rest of the country is not mentioned again but it is worth considering whether the solution devised for the metropolitan county areas could not also apply elsewhere.

Any justification for the different treatment of the metropolitan areas must rest on their distinctiveness from the rest of the country. It is difficult to find geographical criteria which mark out the existing metropolitan county areas. They are not self-contained economic units, nor contiguous built-up areas, nor are they towns with their adjacent hinterlands any more than, say, Cleveland or Humberside. The metropolitan district council areas are even less distinctive. It is difficult, for example, to justify different forms of local government in Warrington and Trafford or in Middlesbrough and Sunderland on the grounds of their geographical characteristics.

The current proposals for 'single-tier' local government are being applied in areas where the government thought, in 1971, there was a need for a strategic authority. The need for strategy, it is now argued, has passed and local government should be concerned with more practical things such as value for money in the delivery of services. A way forward in pursuit of value for money is to do away with an unnecessary tier of administration. This approach could be applied elsewhere. If the shire district councils account for only 13 per cent of expenditure and have relatively few functions, the existence of large numbers of elected members cannot be justified on value for money criteria. Their functions (housing, environmental health, recreation, local planning, a limited amount of highways maintenance, rate collection and a few minor matters) could easily be transferred to the county councils.

It could also be argued that a solution which applies in Wirral or South Tyneside could equally apply in Bristol or Southampton. Towns and cities outside the current metropolitan county areas which were previously county boroughs, have argued consistently that they could be most-purpose authorities again. The existence of single-tier local government in the metropolitan areas revives that case, which was being discussed under the title *Organic Change* by the last Labour government but was rejected after 1979 (see Stewart, Leach and Skelcher, 1979).

The Likely Impact of the Present Proposals

However, the government has opted for a reform which is limited to the metropolitan areas. The proposals were produced in a hurry and lack consistency, but they are an attempt to meet the criticisms of the present system expressed in the White Paper.

The first criticism was that the upper-tier authorities were created in an era when there was 'a certain fashion for strategic planning' (para. 1.3). The White Paper says that priorities are now less theoretical and more practical and have particular regard for value for money. It is certainly the case that the proposed arrangements would militate against strategic planning by local government. The newly proposed land-use planning system would operate under strict influence from the DoE which would provide 'strategic guidance' for the districts and boroughs. Strategy in land-use planning has not gone out of fashion; it would be shifted from the local authorities to the DoE.

A second criticism was that the existing system is too expensive and that the proposed arrangements would be cheaper, although the size of the expected savings has never been revealed. Value for money, or at least a close control on expenditure, would be exercised under the proposed system. The government intends to control spending. In a speech to the Annual General Meeting of the Association of British Chambers of Commerce in May 1984 Patrick Jenkin said: 'the large expenditure and manpower budgets of the joint boards will be subject to limits set by the government for the first three years of their existence. We will be able and intend to exert downward pressure on manpower and expenditure in these areas.' It is not clear whether there is Home Office approval for the downward pressure on manpower in the police and fire services, but the intent of the DoE is clear.

A third criticism of the existing system was that the upper tier has too few service delivery functions and that this causes them to search for a wider strategic role. Since the implementation of strategy calls for co-operation from the lower tier this may bring conflict between the tiers. 'It may also lead them to promote policies which conflict with national policies which are the responsibility of central government' (para. 1.12). The strategic resource allocation role of local government would be weakened by the proposals, since the major areas of spending of the existing MCCs would be controlled by independent bodies responsible only for a single budget. Choices between budgets would, therefore, not take place within a strategic framework.

What would be the result of the proposed structure in these two matters? Outside London there would be public transport undertakings which would take decisions on routes and fares. One of the recent sources of conflict between elements of the lower tier and the upper tier has been over the amount of the precept and the level of fares. This element of conflict would not be removed by the proposals. Indeed if the government proposed to control the level of the public transport precept in such a way as to force fare increases there would be likely to be a great deal of conflict with those lower-tier authorities which support cheap fares for public transport. Other matters over which conflict has arisen include land-use planning, and particularly Green Belt policies. These decisions would still be taken, although now under 'guidance' from the DoE. Conflicts of interest between areas would persist, but the institutions between which the conflict would take place would change.

Conflicts between central and local government would still arise, as there will remain socialist councils which are developing strategic policies on such matters as employment and economic development which are contradictory to government policy. There are also authorities (including some Conservative ones) which oppose the government's spending limits which may also be seen as matters which are the responsibility of central government. It may well be argued that policing and fire cover are matters of central government concern, since they are controlled by the Home Office, although the proposals retain an element of local control through the proposed joint boards.

A fourth improvement which the White Paper claimed was that the proposals 'will ... provide a system which is simpler for the public to understand' (para. 1.19). The existing system is difficult to understand. The overlaps in highways maintenance and planning are confusing as is the split between waste collection and waste disposal.

The differences in the system between metropolitan and other areas are also difficult to understand as witnessed, for example, by references in Conservative Party briefing material for the 1983 general election to Greater Manchester Council's house-building record (Greater Manchester is not a housing authority). It is doubtful, however, whether the multitude of joint boards and joint committees proposed would be more comprehensible than the existing arrangements.

Joint Boards and Joint Committees

How would the proposed statutory and voluntary joint arrangements work? To answer this question it is worth considering the experience of other joint arrangements among local authorities. Two of the present authors have made an examination of such arrangements which has been published elsewhere (Flynn and Leach, 1984). Two types of arrangements are proposed, joint boards and joint committees. A joint board is 'a corporate body, created by order of a Minister, and in many cases requiring the approval of Parliament. It has perpetual succession, a common seal and it can hold land. . . . It has independent financial powers, including the power to borrow and obtain the money it needs from constituent authorities by means of precepts' (C. A. Cross, 1981, pp. 78–9). Joint committees on the other hand have no corporate status independent of their constituent authorities, and cannot hold property, borrow or precept. They are the creatures of the authorities creating them and their constitutions and powers are controlled by the constituent authorities.

The joint boards proposed in the White Paper differ from existing joint boards in three respects. William Waldegrave announced on 17 January 1984 that the members of the boards would be recallable at will by the constituent authorities and would have to reflect the views of those authorities. At the same time the composition of the boards would (proportionately) reflect the parties in the constituent authorities except in London where each borough would send one representative to the fire board. For the first three years of their existence the joint boards would have to gain the approval of the secretary of state for their budgets and their staffing levels.

The principles of recallability and proportional representation are incompatible. The member who does not represent the views of the authority which s/he represents will be subject to recall, although s/he has been chosen to represent the party to which s/he belongs. Members of a council's minority party would be in a difficult position when sitting on a joint board. The third principle, control by the secretary of state over the budget, implies a limited discretion for the joint boards. Already police committees have limited control over the way in which a police force is run by the chief constable and removal of influence over the size of the budget further reduces that control. In the case of fire, Home Office guidelines already provide strict limits within which the fire service is operated. In public transport, a major decision is the degree to which fares are subsidized, a decision which will be severely limited if the overall budget was set by the secretary of state.

Within their limited remit the joint boards would operate in isolation from other services. Key decisions in local government are those which allocate resources among services according to political priorities and perceived needs. The more services are provided by specialist bodies the less scope there is for local consideration of resource allocation. If, for example, the decision on the level of investment in public transport was made in a special joint board, while the decision on the level of road construction was taken by individual district councils, nowhere would an assessment be made of the relative returns to those two investments.

The accountability of the members of the joint boards would be limited. Members elected to a local authority would in turn be nominated to a board. They would not stand for election on a policy statement relating to police, fire or public transport for which they would be held to account. Experience shows that even reporting back to the constituent council is rare from existing joint bodies.

The experience of joint committees has been that they work well when they are set up voluntarily, they have a small number of constituent authorities, the task is well defined and uncontentious, and the function does not involve a great deal of net cost to the constituent authorities. If these conditions are not met the joint committees delay decisions and make decisions which offend nobody rather than ones which provide the best solution to the problem.

In the White Paper, voluntary co-operation, backed by the threat of ministerial intervention, is suggested in waste disposal and planning, and voluntary co-operation is implied in the case of highways and traffic management, arts and recreation, trading standards and consumer protection. Many of these services are contentious, complicated, involve a large number of authorities, and joint working is suggested by the government, while reserve powers are taken to enforce co-operation if it is not achieved voluntarily. They are also issues which involve a clash of interests between councils. The siting of waste disposal plants will continue to cause friction. Many planning decisions such as the siting of new commercial developments, or the protection of Green Belts, are matters which produce winners and losers. In other words the conditions under which voluntary co-operation has been successful in the past are not present in this case and conflicts between authorities would be resolved by the Department of the Environment or the Department of Transport, rather than within local government.

At their worst the proposals for joint provision could mean that police, fire and local public transport will join those other services which have disappeared from control by directly elected local authorities. They could follow the path of the water authorities with decreasing representation of local authorities and an increasing proportion of members nominated by central government. Conversely, police and fire could become the subject of many years of further discussion as district councils prepare their bids to become police and fire authorities, or as new groupings of authorities form consortia to take over these services.

The Next Local Government Reform

These unsatisfactory arrangements, and the fact that there would be serious anomalies between the systems of local government in the metropolitan areas and that in the rest of the country mean that there would be pressure for yet another reform of local government. The current reform is part of a tendency towards centralization. The controls on rate levels give the government unprecedented controls over the budgets of individual local authorities. The arrangements proposed for the replacement of the GLC and the MCCs represent the transfer of the majority of expenditure to bodies whose budgets are under central government control, and imply a high degree of central government influence over other matters. A future reform may arise from a different view of the nature of local government.

A genuine review of local government would include consideration of the relevant grouping of services to be included in a local government body: the boundaries to be adopted; the mechanism for resource allocation, including the questions of the number of tiers of control; source of revenue and the degree to which the local government units should be autonomous. These are all fundamental questions which apply to the whole local government system, though the present debate focuses on the system in metropolitan and other urban areas.

The Relevant Grouping of Services

At the moment there is a spectrum of types of government agencies operating at the local level. At one end there are local offices of central government departments which are funded centrally and are directly accountable to central government. These local offices may have local advisory machinery, such as the Area Manpower Boards of the Manpower Services Commission, but they are not under local control. There are also quangos, such as appointed water authorities, some of whose members may feel answerable locally. At the other end of the spectrum are local-authority-provided services which are controlled by directly elected councillors who are accountable, in principle, to the electorate. The decision about what form of body to create for different services is taken by governments according to how much control they want over the bodies, and the degree to which they desire uniformity across the country. If social security benefits are to be paid at a uniform rate and according to a uniform set of rules, there is little point in having social security payments under local authority administration. (There are exceptions to this rule, such as the payment of housing benefit by local authorities, but that decision was taken in order to limit the number of staff needed in the DHSS.)

On the other hand, if resources are to be allocated in such a way that the best use is made of them, decisions on service provision should be made among as many services as possible. This is as true of decisions about services made in the public sector as it is in the case of market decisions. Elected representatives making choices among social services, housing provision and education balance the benefits of those services against the costs of providing them, at least at the margins. Consumers make the same sort of choice among the goods presented to them. Any restriction in the choice reduces the possibility of the best decisions emerging. This argument leads towards organizations with many responsibilities, rather than special-purpose bodies, and towards the establishment of as few levels of government as possible.

The Relevant Boundaries

Before the last reorganization, much consideration was given to the idea of 'strategic' authorities. It was felt that there were matters which required resolution at a scale smaller than the whole country, but larger than that appropriate for the delivery of such services as refuse collection and housing. These issues included highway and transportation planning, major land-use changes and, possibly, resource allocation. There has also been a long debate about the size of unit which can produce different services efficiently. These issues have never been satisfactorily resolved. As the Redcliffe-Maud Commission said:

It is not possible to derive from the research statistical proof about the best size of authority for any particular service . . . there is no such thing as a single 'right' size for any local government service – but . . . the area of an authority responsible for education, housing and personal services should contain at least a population of around 250,000. (paras 256 and 257)

Our own conclusion is that there is no single service in which administration by a very large authority would have decisive disadvantages. (para. 269)

The existing system is not based on any notion of optimal size of unit. Personal social services are provided by Strathclyde Regional Council for a population of 2·4 million and by the Royal Borough of Kingston upon Thames for a population of 133,700. Housing is provided both by the City of Birmingham for a population of 1,017,300 as well as by Teesdale District Council which has a population of 24,600. It is not clear that unit costs do vary significantly with size, and in any case many of the larger authorities are organized in a decentralized way, with effective administrative units smaller than the whole area. However, to exercise effectively the strategic role discussed in Chapter 2, authorities require large boundaries.

Size is not the only criterion for boundary definition. A criterion which applied the idea of a socio-economic area was applied in Derek Senior's memorandum of dissent to the Redcliffe-Maud Committee. If this notion was adopted the boundaries would be drawn in such a way as to maximize the number of people who lived and worked within the same administrative area. This in turn would fulfil the principle that taxpayers should receive benefits from the tax which they pay and people would pay local taxes in the area in which they lived. Boundaries could be drawn on the basis of class or socio-economic group. Classes could either be segregated or mixed, depending on the preference of the people responsible. A proposal by Ken Young (1984b) to change the boundaries of the London boroughs to group together outer and inner areas would unite administratively their populations. The existing London borough boundaries have created some boroughs which are almost entirely working class, such as Barking and Dagenham and Tower Hamlets. It has also created some very mixed-class boroughs such as Kensington and Chelsea and Merton. Whose interests are better served by the mixing of classes in the same administrative unit and whose interests are served by separation? Some local authority services are primarily used by working-class people, while others produce most benefits for the middle classes. Middle-class people could protect themselves from tax burdens by segregating themselves from people who require local authority support.

Party control of the units created is the politically relevant criterion when decisions on boundaries are made. The inclusion of only inner London in a special education authority increases the probability of Labour control, while allowing the outer London boroughs to be education authorities maximizes the chances of Conservative control over education there. The Birmingham boundary, which excludes the Chelmsley Wood overspill estate which was placed in Solihull and includes the middle-class areas of Sutton Coldfield, has ensured a shifting pattern of power in that city since 1974.

The question of boundaries drawn around socio-economic groups and party supporters is really one of where the conflicts between people are enacted. If a boundary is drawn in such a way as to include members of the whole socio-economic spectrum, then the conflicts between interests can be expressed within a single unit of government, the local authority. If they are drawn in such a way as to segregate the classes, as occurs in the cities in the United States, then the conflicts have no single forum for expression, but occur through inter-organizational conflict which may have its resolution, or its continuance, at another level in the government machine. If the boundaries separate classes of people, it is important to decide whether there should be intermediate tiers of government between central government and the principal unit of local government.

How Many Tiers?

The fundamental questions are: how should resource allocation decisions be made and over what area? The present system of resource allocation has three basic elements: central government decides on the amount of central government grant and how that grant is distributed; local authorities decide their level of expenditure (increasingly influenced and, after rate-capping, limited by central government); within that level of expenditure the authorities decide on the use to which that expenditure will be put, with regard to both the services to be funded and the areas in which they are to be spent. The Herbert Commission suggested that London needed a body which would be responsible for resource distribution and the same argument may be applied to the other conurbations. This is not only a question of resource equalization which can be done relatively mechanically, but also one of allocating priorities to areas and service developments.

The existing system allocates grant according to indicators of the need to spend to provide a standard level of service. These indicators, which make up the grant related expenditure assessment, include demographic indicators and some indication of special needs such as the level of unemployment. Grant is then distributed according to the gap between what is available as local resources (the rateable values in the area) and what is needed to provide a standard level of service. The system therefore takes account both of needs to spend and the resources available locally. Although the calculation is in fact quite crude, with size and age distribution of population the predominant indicators, it does match grant to need to some extent. In addition, there is a London equalization scheme which deals with the problem of the very uneven distribution of rateable values in London. Any mechanism which was established to fit between the central government and local authorities would not therefore necessarily have to deal with the overall equalization aspect. But is there a role for a system which sets priorities for expenditure at a lower level? Is there a case for a system of resource allocation within the urban areas which would, for example, assess the needs to spend in the inner urban areas because of social stress and/or older infrastructure which requires additional maintenance and repairs expenditure? If there is a need for such a mechanism, how should the decision-making process work, what should be the method of choosing the decision-makers and how should they be accountable? These are the questions to be answered before consideration of an upper tier is made. An upper tier which is not responsible for resource allocation would find it difficult to establish a strategic role.

This function has to be carried out somewhere and it involves real material interests of the people in the areas to which resources are allocated. The present system leaves the last word in the resolution of conflicting interests between areas with the secretary of state through his control over the grant mechanism and formula. The formula is open to scrutiny and the elements in it are subject to argument, but there is no accountability from the secretary of state back to local government about the way in which the formula is used. This question is even more important when the level above which rates are capped is set using the existing grant related expenditure formula, which now determines not only the grant distribution, but also the level of expenditure.

Three choices are available: continue the existing grant distribution system; change to a national grant distribution system which deals only with resource equalization (and therefore reduces in scale); leave the distribution of grant (within an overall total set by central government) to local government. If the last were chosen the question is whether there should be a hierarchical distribution, with grant allocated first to regions by some national mechanism, and then within the regions by some regional mechanism. It is not at all obvious that there should be a regional mechanism. It could be argued that the priorities for expenditure between, say, Solihull and Dudley could as easily be considered along with those between Solihull and Knowsley, as taken at regional level, if criteria are used which can be applied mechanically. If local knowledge is needed in the judgements, then consideration needs to be given to an intermediate tier. An intermediate tier also has the possibility of some form of local accountability.

What Options are Available?

The range of answers available to these questions produces a wide variety of options for the local government system. Indeed, within the United Kingdom, there are already at least seven different distributions of functions. In Scotland the regional authorities provide the majority of services, including education, social services, transportation, highways and water, while the lower tier are mainly housing authorities. The distribution of functions is uniform throughout the country, except in the Western Isles which is a unitary authority. In Northern Ireland almost all the services are provided by the Northern Ireland Executive. In England there are different distributions of functions in inner and outer London and in the metropolitan and shire counties. Theoretically, there are many different ways of organising the delivery of public services at the local level but three broad options stand out as politically viable.

1   *Unitary authorities of relatively autonomous units controlling the maximum feasible number of services*

This is the Jones and Stewart (1983) ideal type, where the local government system is made up of a set of local authorities which would be the only elected level of government other than Parliament. They would, in their case, have populations of between 150,000 and 500,000 (although larger units could be created in exceptional circumstances), would perform all the existing functions of local government and would have in addition the functions of the Department of Health and Social Security (DHSS), Department of Employment and Manpower Services Commission. There would be central grants used for the purpose of equalizing income, but there would be a clear constitutional separation of central and local government. Any services or strategic control which needed to be exercised at a higher than local level would be done by co-operation between the basic units of local government. There would be no intermediate tier between local and central government because this would reduce the comprehensibility of the system.

A variation would be to establish unitary authorities at the conurbation-wide level, eliminating the district and borough councils. Since such authorities would cover a very large area, it is likely that services would be organized in a decentralized way. It would then follow that control and accountability should also be decentralized, which would result in the establishment of a lower tier within the conurbation-wide authority.

With real local autonomy boundaries become the determinants of which interests are in the majority. Real autonomy implies the capture of the authority by a set of interests. The 'community', with a consensus of opinion about the best way forward for 'community government', would in fact be governed by majority rule according to where the boundaries were drawn.

2 Local administration of centrally controlled services

At the other end of the spectrum there could be a system of administration which did away with the need for any elected tier of government other than Westminster. If living in a unitary state implies a uniform level of service throughout the country there is no scope for local choice. Rate-capping implies that eventually local authorities will have no discretion to exceed the level of expenditure set by the government. The permitted level will be based on a formula of needs assessment. Since in its present form that assessment makes the expenditure requirements for particular services explicit, the elements already exist for a nationally determined service to be administered in all areas. All that is required to move further along that road is the abolition of the remaining local authorities.

Each service could be run by independent agencies. Already health, water, social security, employment offices, manpower services commission, housing associations, sports councils, the Arts Council, and so on are independent agencies operating under overall control from the centre. A national curriculum with central employment of teachers and lecturers would establish a national education system. (In Italy and France, for example, teachers are paid directly by central government although education is administered locally.) Such a national education system would allow much more complete ministerial control over the standard of educational provision and the content of the education process. The sale of council houses and the virtual disappearance of new municipal house-building for general needs could lead to the public housing service becoming a residual function catering for only the poorest tenants in the most basic property. Other sectors of the rented market could be controlled by housing associations. If the size of housing association stock reached that of the local authority stock, then they could relatively easily take over the management. Such a move could take place under the banner of competition and tendering for the housing management functions, with private companies and housing associations bidding to take on the management function from local authorities. Social services provision could be run by voluntary agencies and the private sector (particularly in the case of the care of the elderly) with a regulatory body responsible for licensing and maintenance of standards of provision. That element of social services provision which is concerned with offenders could be transferred to the courts and provided nationally, along with the national prosecuting service. Refuse collection and disposal could be run by a separate management body using the services of private contractors.

3   An intermediate tier

There are various versions of the intermediate tier solution. Certain elements of the Labour Party adopt a contradictory position favouring both unitary local authorities and regional government. The Social Democratic and Liberal parties both favour some form of regional government, grouping together those elements of central government departments which operate at the regional level (such as the Department of Industry and Department of the Environment) and putting them under the control of an elected regional assembly.

Another version of the intermediate tier is the strengthening of the existing upper tier in the metropolitan areas and in London. The current administration at the GLC, for example, is in favour of that body taking over health provision in the capital and establishing control of the Metropolitan Police. The addition of a resource allocation role and the restoration of a powerful housing role to the GLC would create an institution with power to adopt a strategic role in relation to the development of the city and the provision of public services. In the areas currently covered by the MCCs, the GLC and possibly other areas such as South Hampshire, a solution similar to the Scottish model would be possible. Here the major services would be provided by the upper tier, with the lower tier taking only residual functions. If housing was to be reduced to a service of last resort, it could be carried out in conjunction with social services at the upper tier.

A weak version is the model which includes a regional assembly with few executive powers. The Conservative group in the present GLC have proposed such a solution for London, as has Roland Freeman, former chairman of the GLC finance committee and now a member of the SDP (see *New Democrat*, Jan./Feb. 1984). The function of such assemblies would be discussion of services and some notion of 'co-ordination' of services.

Criteria for Choice

In considering a future reorganization, what criteria should be applied to the choices which have to be made? *Streamlining the Cities* offered no explicit criteria for a local government system, apart from some criticisms of the existing system, although the implied criteria may be found in the proposals themselves and would include the merits of a single tier of administration and the need for central influence over the major services. The problem with establishing general criteria against which to judge an existing or proposed local government system is that the nature of the judgement depends on who is making it. Central government may have very different requirements from those of local government. The users of local authority services may prefer forms of government which do not meet the interests of those charged with providing the services.

Fundamentally, the criteria applied by a central government would concern whether the system had characteristics which give the requisite degree of central control and whether it allowed social policy to be pursued in the way government required. Within those overall requirements there would then be criteria relating to the efficiency of the system in pursuing the government's objectives. Political parties in government would also have political criteria relating to the possibilities of a particular party maintaining control of local authorities, and of the interests which those parties represent achieving sufficient influence over local authority activities.

From the point of view of the users of the service, the main criteria concern the degree to which the system produces the services which they want as efficiently as possible including both the requirements that local authorities should be able to allocate their resources in such a way as to generate the most possible benefits (allocative efficiency) and that they should produce the chosen services at the least possible cost (productive efficiency).

The local government system should also be comprehensible to the citizen. Comprehensibility implies that it should be clear which organization is responsible for the delivery of services. Opinion polls have shown that the present system is not well understood and that people are confused both about which local government services are provided by which tier and about which services are provided by health authorities and other central government agencies. It is not surprising that such confusion exists. The citizen is faced with a myriad of agencies providing services: DHSS, Department of Employment, health authority, Citizens Advice Bureau, district and county councils and water authorities all provide everyday services. Comprehensibility is also about understanding how decisions are made about what service to deliver and the standards to which they are to be provided, as a prerequisite to participating in those decisions. The present system is opaque, especially at the level of understanding how resources are allocated among, say, health and local authorities. Even within individual agencies the decision-making process is difficult to understand, and the concerned citizen attempting to take an interest in all the decision-making within and between agencies would find him or herself faced with a full-time occupation of investigation and questioning. Comprehensibility also requires the citizen to understand the process of access to services. The present fragmented nature of welfare state provision makes accessibility difficult and results in the under-use of many available services.

A second general criterion is accountability. In a parliamentary democracy the normal form of accountability is through the electoral process. A local system of government should allow for the accountability of service providers and agencies of control and regulation to the local electorate. In the present system the degree of local accountability is varied. Some local agencies, particularly those controlled by local authorities, are in principle directly accountable to the electorate. Others, which are controlled by nominated local authority members, are indirectly accountable, while those which are run as quangos or are controlled by central government have no local accountability at all. Regional offices of central government departments, such as the Departments of Industry, the Environment and Health and Social Security, have no lines of accountability to the local electorate. Accountability is not simply a question of a formal procedure of producing reports and accounts, but is also a question of explaining and being held responsible for actions taken or not taken.

The criteria of the service consumer also include the requirement that the agencies of government at local level should be able to respond to the changing needs and demands of the people. The services provided will differ according to the degree to which particular classes or groups are in control at the local level, but there are certain prerequisites for responsiveness. The agency should be in a position to allocate resources to particular activities among competing demands. The agencies require a capacity for assessing needs and eliciting demands. Fragmentation of agencies makes this responsiveness harder to achieve. Water authorities are able to assess the demand for water and for sewerage services. Planning authorities are able to gauge the demand for development land. Education authorities are able to assess the need for education services. The DHSS is able to assess the need for social security payments. Each agency has the task of assessing the requirements of its own clients. Resource allocation among competing demands requires that there is a mechanism of choice which allows priorities to be established. This is a very difficult task within local government since the budget process which allocates resources among, say, housing, education and social services is constrained by vested interests and inertia, but at least adjustments can be made over time. Expenditure on education can be adjusted downwards as the child population reduces, while the expenditure on care for the elderly can be adjusted upwards as the numbers of elderly people increase. Once the resource allocation decisions are removed from a single agency the reallocation becomes more difficult and more remote from the local people. Cabinet decisions on the allocation of expenditure between Department of Industry and Manpower Services Commission cannot possibly take account of the effectiveness of those expenditures at local level. High-level decisions about the allocation of expenditure for elderly people among hospitals, social services and housing are not likely to achieve the best possible value for the money spent.

How do these criteria help in the choice among the major structural options? No single solution emerges because the preferred system depends on who is making the choice, but such an analysis may help to predict the shape of the local government system and its effectiveness.

From the point of view of a central government which wishes to exercise a high degree of control, the first option is attractive only if there is consensus about the nature of social policy. Autonomy implies that different authorities would behave in different ways. We have seen that a major element in the current proposals is the desire to prevent local authorities from adopting positions and policies which are contrary to those of the government.

On the other hand, the existence of only one tier would eliminate duplication and would provide the possibility of an efficient production of services. Whether such a system would meet political objectives would depend on how the boundaries were drawn. Our discussion of the options of separating or combining socio-economic groups has shown that there is a choice to be made which could give different results in electoral terms.

As far as the user of services is concerned, the unitary local government unit on a relatively small scale gives a good result. Since most relevant services would be provided by a single body it could be comprehensible to the citizen. Choices about resource allocation would be made across a wide range of services, and since they would be made for a relatively small area the decisions could be open to scrutiny. A conurbation-wide unitary authority, however, would be more remote.

The second option, of locally administered, centrally controlled services, would be attractive to a central government confident that its policies were appropriate and that there was the capacity for adequate administrative control from the centre. Independent agencies reporting directly to central government departments and operating to a set of centrally determined rules are more easy to control than a set of relatively independent local bodies.

From the citizen's point of view such a system has few attractions, unless the central government is operating in his or her interests. From the point of view of, say, business interests in a predominantly working-class locality, such a system would offer protection. However, it offers very little local accountability, accessibility and comprehensibility. Nor would it offer any local choices over the allocation of resources, since centrally determined programmes and policies would be applied uniformly, allowing no possibility of local responsiveness.

Whose interests would be served by the existence of an intermediate tier of government? Politically the question can be answered only in relation to a particular set of boundaries and a particular set of functions at the intermediate level. A strong intermediate tier with the powers to reallocate resources between rich and poor areas could act in the interests of either set of areas, depending on where the political balance lay. A widely drawn London boundary, for example, could produce an intermediate tier which acted always in the interests of the suburban areas at the expense of the residents of the inner city. A weak intermediate tier would simply provide a forum for the debate about resource distribution and policy direction of the tier below.

On the other hand, the lack of an intermediate tier leaves resource allocation in the hands of central government. Resources competition between, say, inner and outer areas of the conurbations cannot be resolved by boroughs which each cover only one sort of area. Redistribution or equalization has to be done at some higher level, and disputes cannot necessarily be resolved by agreement.

From the consumer's point of view an intermediate tier is not necessarily more remote, especially if it is providing services in a decentralized way. The education authority is not necessarily less accessible to pupils or parents in the shire counties than it is in the metropolitan districts. However, if services are distributed between tiers, resource allocation becomes more difficult because it is more effective to have the choice between services made within one authority than in two separate ones.

An authority at a conurbation-wide scale offers some solutions to the problems posed by the others. Resource allocation choices can be made both among services and among areas containing different socio-economic groups, within a single authority. Such a solution implies that the boundaries would contain a wide variety of types of areas and thus the tensions between poor and rich areas would be expressed within a single institution. From a central government's point of view, political control would be the key issue, since it raises the possibility of Conservative control over some services in, say, Sheffield or Manchester or conversely Labour control of outer suburban areas now consistently Conservative.

It is difficult to imagine the circumstances in which a central government of any party would create genuinely autonomous local authorities and allow them to follow their own version of social policy. Over the last decade there has been a polarization of local politics. Major policy differences now exist not just between but within parties. There are Conservative local administrations which believe strongly in rolling back the boundaries of the state and the extension of the market mechanism as a resource allocation system into areas which have been outside the market since the Second World War. There are those in the Labour Party who believe in the establishment of collective provision of many of those things which are now distributed through the market mechanism. There is no longer strong consensual agreement about the method of decision-making or the nature of the services to be provided. Because of this, governments of the right or left are unlikely to be willing to allow local authorities to go their own way, but are more likely to wish to control, or at least heavily influence, the major policy choices of local authorities.

The administrative forms produced by the next reorganization will be determined by the party which is in power at the time. Support for the Labour Party is more concentrated than that of the other parties and it is disadvantageous to Labour to have its supporters absorbed within very large units. The SDP–Liberal Alliance has very evenly spread support and could hope to gain a significant number of seats in most urban areas only through proportional representation. The Conservative Party gains advantages from combining middle-class, Conservative areas with the Labour enclaves.

It would be in Labour's interests to create relatively small local government units where its support could be almost guaranteed, at least in the urban areas. Having established a fairly high probability of control, the local government units should, from this standpoint, be given as many powers as is administratively feasible.

A future Conservative government could try to absorb the Labour support into wider areas, whose boundaries are drawn in such a way as to ensure Conservative control. An alternative strategy would be to follow the pattern of the USA where poor areas are allowed a relatively high degree of political autonomy within tightly defined boundaries and with little financial help from federal government. The choice depends on the strategy adopted towards the inner city areas. It is possible to predict the social policy framework within which a future local government reform would take place in Britain's urban areas, if a government with a philosophy similar to that of the present administration were in office.

Public expenditure would be limited, not just because of the availability of resources but because of a commitment to the reduction of the proportion of the national product which is allocated to public expenditure. If services have to be provided or supervised by public authorities there would be pressure to ensure that as much of the production of the services as possible is carried out by private companies.

Steps would be taken to ensure that the national interest, which is interpreted mainly as the interests of the business sector, will be protected. Services would be geared towards the needs of business, particularly the education service and the provision of infrastructure. Self-reliance and the strengthening of the family as the basic unit of welfare provision would be promoted as the alternative to state provision. There will be a presumption that care will be provided by the family, by private insurance or by the voluntary sector with state provision available only as a last resort.

The social environment in which services are provided will probably be harsher. Economic forecasts suggest that even with a successful recovery in the economy unemployment will remain high. The unemployed are likely to be unevenly distributed both geographically and socially, the centres of the cities having a disproportionate share of the unemployed and the ethnic minorities being hardest hit. Demographic change will result in an increasing proportion of the population being old.

The move towards privatization of housing provision will result in the public sector housing which remains being occupied by poor people who are unable to take advantage of owner-occupation. This will result in concentrations of poor people in the housing estates which are not sold to their tenants. Many poor people will also be owner-occupiers with incomes inadequate to provide maintenance of their houses when they become unemployed or retire. Reductions in public expenditure will result in deterioration of other aspects of the infrastructure and environment. In these circumstances, it may be politically advantageous for the Conservatives to leave the inner city area under Labour control since the inner city local authorities could be then held responsible for the deterioration.

It is quite likely, then, that both the Conservative and Labour parties would favour a local government system in the urban areas which had limited local autonomy and which separated the inner and outer areas. Central government, of either party, would wish to maintain control of the main thrust of social policy and each party has good reason to isolate the areas of Labour support from the rest.

The only likely contradiction of this pattern would be a future coalition government between Labour or Conservative parties and the SDP-Liberal Alliance. The price for Alliance support is likely to be a move towards proportional representation in the voting system, and its introduction into local elections is a likely compromise agreement. The political calculations would then change with proportional representation on a conurbation-wide scale likely to give the Alliance the maximum chance of holding the balance of power in the urban areas. Hence, if such a coalition were to produce a reform of local government, it may well opt for a two-tier system with some powers and services at a geographical level which is larger than the existing MCCs and would be introduced under the banner of 'regional government'.

A Unitary State

It is clear that the changes which are being debated now consist simply of the abolition of a set of institutions and do not represent a thorough, considered reform of the local government system. The alternative arrangements which are proposed were hurriedly constructed and were subject to quite major changes after the publication of the White Paper. The decision to abolish the GLC and the MCCs was itself taken as an expedient before the 1983 general election. These changes do not represent a lasting solution to the problems of the local government system. Indeed uncertainty about the future is inherent in the proposal that the police and fire services should possibly be subject to another administrative change in a few years. A further source of uncertainty is the creation of most-purpose authorities in the 'metropolitan' areas which would surely increase the pressure from the ex-county boroughs in the rest of the country to be given equivalent status and powers.

The uncertainty about the future shape of the local government system is compounded by the increasing uncertainty about the financial future. The introduction of targets for expenditure and grant penalties for exceeding those targets prevented authorities from predicting their income. Presistent changes to the rules have made medium-term financial service planning almost impossible. The rules by which rate-capping will be applied are also subject to the whim of the secretary of state, with no protection for local authorities.

The combined effects of these two sources of uncertainty must be to weaken the institutions of local government. If the next reform is carried out by a government which wishes to strengthen those institutions, it will have to include measures which give some stability and predictability. At the very least, the need for further reform should not be inherent in the next reorganization. If there is to be local autonomy, then it should be clearly defined and the rules about the relations between central and local government should be codified. The changes to the financial system and the abolition of the GLC and the MCCs show that the institutions of local government in Britain have no constitutional protection from the centre. Britain has been shown to be a unitary state and this has allowed central government a free hand in manipulating the system to meet its own political objectives.

References

Abercrombie, L. P. (1945), *The Greater London Plan: 1944* (London: HMSO).

Alexander, A. (1982), *Local Government in Britain since Reorganisation* (London: Allen & Unwin).

Boddy, M. and Fudge, C. (eds) (1984), *Local Socialism* (London: Macmillan).

Bridges, L. and Vielba, C. (1976), *Structure Plan Examinations in Public: a Descriptive Analysis* (University of Birmingham: Institute of Judicial Administration).

Bristow, M. R. (1984), *A Response to 'Streamlining the Cities'* (London: Regional Studies Association, mimeo).

Bristow, S. (1978), 'Local politics after reorganisation: the homogenisation of local government in England and Wales', *Public Administration Bulletin*, no. 28, pp. 17–33.

Bristow, S., Kermode, D. and Mannin, M. (1984), *The Redundant Counties? Participation and Electoral Choice in England's Metropolitan Counties* (Ormskirk, Lancs: G. W. & A. Hesketh).

Calderwood, R. (1984), 'The role of the upper tier in England and Scotland: a comparison', in S. N. Leach (ed.), *The Future of Metropolitan Government*.

CIPFA (1984), *Local Government: Comparative Statistics*.

Confederation of British Industry (1983), *The Reform of Local Government in the Metropolitan Areas: Submission to the Secretary of State for the Environment*.

Coopers and Lybrand Associates (1983), *'Streamlining the Cities': an Analysis of the Government's Case for Reorganising Local Government in the Six Metropolitan Counties*.

Coopers and Lybrand Associates (1984), *'Streamlining the Cities': an Analysis of the Costs Involved in the Government's Proposals*.

Cousins, P. (1982), 'The GLC election, 1981', *London Journal*, vol. 8, summer.

Crawford, C. and Moore, V. (1983), *The Free Two Pence* (CIPFA).

Cross, C. A. (1981), *Principles of Local Government Law* (London: Sweet & Maxwell).

Cross, D. T. and Bristow, M. R. (eds) (1983), *English Structure Planning: a Commentary on Procedure and Practice in the Seventies* (London: Pion).

Crossman, R. (1975), *The Diaries of a Cabinet Minister Vol. One: Minister of Housing, 1964–66* (London: Hamish Hamilton/Cape).

Darke, R. (1980), 'The South Yorkshire Structure Plan: examination in public', *Policy and Politics*, vol. 8, no. 2.

DeGrove, J. M. (1977), *The Reorganisation of Local Government in England 1972–77: an Assessment* (Council for International Urban Liaison).

Department of the Environment (1972), *Circular 131/72 Arrangements for the Discharge of Functions ('Agency Arrangements')*.

Department of the Environment (1975), *Circular 74/73 Town and Country Planning: Co-operation between authorities*.

Department of the Environment (1979), *Organic Change in Local Government* (Cmnd 7457, HMSO).

Department of the Environment (1983), *Streamlining the Cities* (Cmnd 9063, HMSO).

Department of the Environment (1983), *Streamlining the Cities: Consultation Papers*
  (a) Reallocation of Transport. Responsibilities in (i) the Greater London Council (ii) Metropolitan County Council Areas.
  (b) The Reallocation of Planning Functions in (i) Greater London Council (ii) Metropolitan County Council Areas.
  (c) Arrangements to be made for Waste Disposal.
  (d) Housing.
  (e) Support for the Arts.

Department of the Environment (1984), *Abolition of the Greater London Council and the Metropolitan County Councils; the Government's Proposals for Transferring Functions to London Boroughs and Metropolitan Districts.*

Dixon, E. S. (1978), *Management in Local Government in West Yorkshire* (University of Bradford: MSocSc thesis).

Dunleavy, P. (1980), *Urban Political Analysis* (London: Macmillan).

Eversley, D. (1984), 'Does London need strategic planning?', *London Journal*, vol. 10, no. 1, summer.

Flynn, N. (1984), *Markets, Hierarchies and Highways Maintenance: the Organisation of Highways Administration in Britain* (University of Birmingham: INLOGOV, mimeo).

Flynn, N. and Leach, S. N. (1984), *Joint Boards and Joint Committees: an Evaluation* (University of Birmingham: INLOGOV).

Greater London Group (1984), *Streamlining the Cities: Proposals for Reorganising Local Government in London and the Metropolitan Counties* (London School of Economics).

Gwilliam, K. M., May, A. D. and Bonsall, P. W. (1984), *Transport in the Metropolitan Counties: Current Performance and Future Prospects* (University of Leeds: Institute of Transport Studies).

Herbert Commission (1960), *Report of the Royal Commission on Local Government in Greater London* (London: HMSO).

House of Commons Environment Committee (1983), *Report 1982–83: the Problems of Urban Renewal in Merseyside.*

Hughes, R. V. (1979), *Fellow Travellers: Inter-Authority Relationships in the West Midlands: an Examination of the Highways Agency Arrangements 1974–79* (University of Birmingham: MSocSc thesis).

INLOGOV (1977), *Management Systems in Local Government: the Two-Tier System* (University of Birmingham: INLOGOV, mimeo).

Isaac-Henry, K. (1984), 'Taking stock of the local authority associations', *Public Administration*, vol. 62, no. 2, summer.

Jones, G. and Stewart, J. D. (1983), *The Case for Local Government* (London: Allen & Unwin).

Keegan, William (1984), *Mrs Thatcher's Economic Experiment* (London: Allen Lane).

Kenny, S. A. and McEvoy, D. (1983), *'Streamlining the Cities': an Examination of the Case for Metropolitan County Government on*

Merseyside. Supplementary Report: Analysis of Merseyside Opinion Survey, November 1983 (Merseyside County Council).

Leach, B. (1985), 'The government of the English provincial conurbations', *Local Government Studies* (forthcoming).

Leach, S. N. (1981), 'The politics of inner city partnerships and programmes, *Local Government Policy Making*, vol. 8, no. 3, spring.

Leach, S. N. (ed.) (1984), *The Future of Metropolitan Government* (University of Birmingham: INLOGOV).

Leach, S. N., Flynn, N. and Vielba, C. (1985), *The Two-Tier System in England and Wales: Report of a Research Project* (University of Birmingham: INLOGOV).

Leach, S. N. and Moore, N. (1979), 'County/district relations in shire and metropolitan counties in the field of town and country planning: a comparison', *Policy and Politics*, vol. 7, no. 2, pp. 165–79.

Lee, J. M., Wood, B. *et al.* (1974), *The Scope of Local Initiative* (London: Martin Robertson).

Local Government Chronicle (1984), Report on ADC Conference no. 6109 6 July 1984, p. 773.

Loughlin, M. (1983), *Local Government, The Law and the Constitution* (Local Government Legal Society Trust).

Marshall, F. (1978), *The Marshall Inquiry on Greater London: Report to Greater London Council* (GLC).

Maund, R. (1982), 'The Greater Manchester adventure: an exercise in strategic environmental improvement', *Environmental Education and Information*, vol. 2, no. 2.

Mawson, J. (1983), *Local Authority Economic Policies in West Yorkshire, 1974–77: an Organisational Perspective* (University of Birmingham: Centre for Urban and Regional Studies Occasional Paper no. 8).

Metropolitan Counties of Greater Manchester, Merseyside, Tyne and Wear, West Yorkshire, South Yorkshire, West Midlands (1984), *Joint Response of the Six Metropolitan Counties to 'Streamlining the Cities'*.

MORI (1980), *Public Opinion in Southwark: Views about the Council and its Activities* (for Southwark London Borough Council).

Norton, A. (1983), *The Government and Administration of Metropolitan Areas in Western Democracies* (University of Birmingham: INLOGOV).

Pauley, R. (1984), 'The politics of local government reorganisation', in S. N. Leach (ed.), *The Future of Metropolitan Government*.

Phillips, H. S. (1945), 'The Abercrombie Greater London Plan', *Public Administration* Vol. 23, p. 38.

Raine, J. (ed.) (1983), *The Fight for Local Government* (University of Birmingham: INLOGOV).

Redcliffe-Maud Commission (1969), *Report of the Royal Commission on Local Government in England 1966–69* (Cmnd 4140, HMSO).

Redcliffe-Maud, Lord and Wood, B. (1974), *English Local Government Reformed* (London: Oxford University Press).

Rhodes, G. (ed.) (1970), *The Government of London: the Struggle for Reform* (London: Wiedenfeld & Nicholson).

Rhodes, G. (ed.) (1972), *The Government of London: The First Five Years* (London: Wiedenfeld & Nicholson).

Rhodes, R. A. W., Hardie, B. and Pudney, N. (1982), *The Reorganisation of*

Local Government and the National Community of Local Government: a Case Study of Organic Change (Colchester: Department of Government, University of Essex, Discussion Paper no. 4).

Richards, P. (1956), *Delegates in Local Government* (London: Allen & Unwin).

Saunders, P. (1979), *Urban Politics: A Sociological Interpretation* (London: Hutchinson).

School for Advanced Urban Studies (1983), *The Future of Local Democracy* (University of Bristol: SAUS).

Skelcher, C. K., Hinings, C. R., Leach, S. N. and Ranson, P. S. (1983), 'Central–local linkages: the impact of policy planning systems', *Journal of Public Policy*, vol. 3, no. 4, pp. 419–34.

Smallwood, F. (1965), *Greater London: The Politics of Metropolitan Reform* (New York: Bobbs-Merrill).

Spence, N. *et al.* (1983), *British Cities: an Analysis of Urban Change* (Oxford: Pergamon).

Stafford, B. (1983), *Water Authorities' Planning Processes* (University of Birmingham: PhD thesis).

Stewart, J. D. (1980), 'Inter-organisational relationships: an introduction', *Town Planning Review*, vol. 51, no. 3, pp. 257–60.

Stewart, J. D. (1983), *Local Government: the Conditions of Local Choice* (London: Allen & Unwin).

Stewart, J. D. (1984), 'The conditions of joint action', *London Journal*, vol. 10, no. 1, pp. 59–65.

Stewart, J. D., Leach, S. N. and Skelcher, C. K. (1979), *Organic Change: a Report on Constitutional Management and Financial Problems* (Association of County Councils).

Stodart Committee (1981), *Report of the Committee of Inquiry into Local Government in Scotland* (Cmnd 8115, HMSO).

Swaffield, J. (1984), *Governing London – Urban Management* (Paper presented to the Governing London Conference, London School of Economics).

Travers, T. (1984), *Local Government Finance in Greater London* (Paper presented to the Governing London Conference, London School of Economics).

Ullswater Commission (1923), *Royal Commission on London Government* (Cmnd 1830, HMSO).

Webb, A. and Wistow, G. (1983), 'Public expenditure and policy implementation: the case of community care', *Public Administration*, vol. 61, spring, pp. 21–44.

West Yorkshire Passenger Transport Executive (1984), *Response to 'Streamlining the Cities'* (West Yorkshire PTE).

Wistrich, E. (1972), *Local Government Reorganisation: the First Five Years of Camden* (London Borough of Camden).

Wood, B. (1976), *The Process of Local Government Reform 1966–74* (London: Allen & Unwin).

Young, K. (ed.) (1975), *Essays on the Study of Urban Politics* (London: Macmillan).

Young, K. (1984a), 'Metropolitan government: the development of the concept and the reality', in S. N. Leach (ed.), *The Future of Metropolitan Government*.

Young, K. (1984b), 'Governing Greater London: the background to GLC abolition and an alternative approach', *London Journal*, vol. 10, no. 1, summer.

Young, K. and Garside, P. (1982), *Metropolitan London: Politics and Urban Change 1837–1981* (London: Edward Arnold).

Young, K. and Kramer, J. (1978), *Strategy and Conflict in Metropolitan Housing* (London: Heinemann).

Appendix 1

Summary of White Paper proposals of the reallocation of functions

FUNCTIONS TO BE TRANSFERRED TO BOROUGH AND DISTRICT COUNCILS

Planning including minerals planning and derelict land reclamation
Highways and traffic management
Waste regulation and disposal
Housing
Trading standards and related functions
Support for the arts
Sport
Historic buildings
Civil defence and emergencies
Support and funding for the magistrates' courts service and the probation
    service
Coroners
School crossing patrols
Building control
Tourism
Entertainments licensing
Archives and libraries
Recreation, parks, and Green Belt land
Safety of sports grounds
Registration of common land and town or village greens
Maps etc in relation to rights of way
Gypsy sites

In a number of cases the borough and district councils already have statutory
powers similar to those of the GLC and MCCs.

FUNCTIONS REQUIRING STATUTORY JOINT ARRANGEMENTS

Police in the Metropolitan Counties
Fire
Education in inner London
Public Transport in the Metropolitan Counties

The MCCs' interests in airports will be transferred to the new public
transport joint boards.

FUNCTIONS REQUIRING OTHER ARRANGEMENTS

Land drainage and flood protection in London will become the responsibility of the Thames Water Authority.

Certain arts sponsorship will be taken over by the Trustees of national museums and galleries.

Smallholdings estates will be transferred to appropriate shire county councils. The function will no longer be carried out by authorities in metropolitan areas.

Source: Streamlining the Cities, Annex B, Department of the Environment (1983).

Appendix 2

Net current expenditure on local authority functions in Greater London metropolitan areas and shire areas – 1983/4 estimates of total grant and rate-borne expenditure.

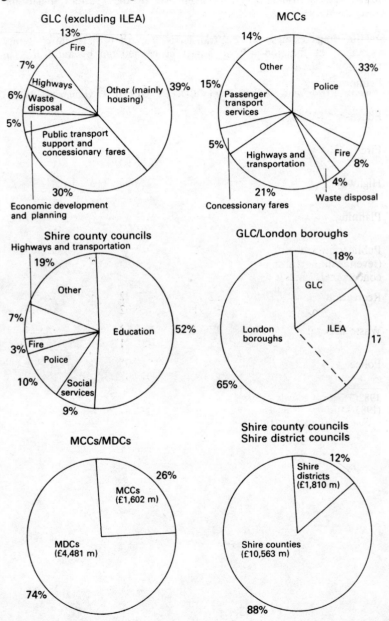

Appendix 3

1982/3 and 1983/4 County Expenditure per capita on Services in the Metropolitan Areas

Service area	GLC	Metropolitan county councils	English non-metropolitan county councils
Economic development	£0·71 (£5·64)	£1·46 (£1·09)	£0·44 (£0·47)
Education (ILEA)	£323·25 (£359·26)	— —	£220·77 (£219·68)
Fire	£15·77 (£16·61)	£11·79 (£11·82)	£9·45 (£9·46)
Highways	£7·39 (£8·21)	£26·03 (£26·60)	£22·56 (£22·00)
Planning	£0·84 (£1·29)	£1·09 (£1·24)	£1·37 (£1·48)
Public transport (revenue support and concessionary fares)	£38·81 (£41·17)	£28·97 (£26·38)	£3·21 (£3·28)
Recreation	£2·43 (£1·91)	£0·22 (£0·02)	£0·44 (£0·18)
Waste disposal	£7·02 (£7·92)	£5·13 (£5·91)	£3·24 (£3·40)
Police	— —	£46·05 (£48·02)	£37·03 (£38·22)

1982/3 figures = actuals
(1983/4) figures = estimates
Source: CIPFA *Local Government Comparative Statistics* (1984).

Appendix 4

Expenditure Comparisons within Metropolitan County Councils (per capita: 1982/3 actuals and 1983/4 estimates)

MCC/	Highways	Police	Service area Planning and development	Waste disposal	Economic development	Fire	Public transport	Total expenditure
Greater Manchester	22·31 (23·10)	48·69 (50·22)	1·10 (1·03)	6·87 (8·24)	0·69 (0·43)	12·00 (11·72)	25·09 (—)	130·04 (134·35)
Merseyside	28·06 (32·64)	57·53 (60·61)	0·73 (1·49)	3·76 (5·48)	1·75 (1·67)	13·97 (14·39)	32·02 (32·56)	165·41 (171·01)
South Yorkshire	30·85 (29·07)	39·58 (41·24)	1·62 (1·83)	2·88 (2·89)	1·57 (1·69)	11·37 (11·09)	54·47 (51·98)	164·27 (160·62)
Tyne and Wear	23·68 (25·38)	42·97 (45·08)	1·73 (1·78)	5·58 (5·57)	2·79 (2·79)	12·62 (12·60)	44·00 (30·87)	134·07 (123·49)
West Midlands	21·86 (21·57)	43·39 (45·20)	0·85 (0·86)	5·38 (5·85)	0·20 (0·70)	10·18 (10·50)	17·27 (15·34)	120·47 (124·64)
West Yorkshire	28·16 (27·85)	43·56 (45·65)	0·95 (1·15)	4·80 (5·43)	3·04 (0·66)	11·84 (11·82)	22·20 (20·22)	129·59 (133·09)
Average	26·03 (26·60)	46·05 (48·02)	1·09 (1·24)	5·13 (5·91)	1·46 (1·09)	11·79 (11·82)	28·97 (18·07)	

Source: CIPFA Local Government Comparative Statistics (1984)

Index

Index